THE PARTNERSHIP: SURVIVING & THRIVING

130 Stories, Strategies, and Practical Tips for Parents and Guardians to Build Positive Relationships with Schools and Support Their Children

ANDREW MAROTTA

EduMatch Publishing

CONTENTS

This book is dedicated to my parents, Dorothy and Joseph Marotta, as well as my in-laws, Patricia and Eugene Grimes, who also have always treated me as their son. I am so blessed and fortunate to have these adults in my life as parents. They have shown me love and support by always having my best interests, and those of my family, in their hearts. They have been there for me in the good times and in bad. For so many of the stories and experiences that I share in this book, I give credit to them. My parents, all four of them, are people of character, love, and family commitment above all else. I thank them for passing these virtues onto me. I hope to be half the parent to my children that they have been to theirs.

Introduction

This book is for you. Yes, you. And me. After my many years of successful experiences of interacting with parents in my office, hallways, and classrooms as Principal at Port Jervis High School in Port Jervis, NY, I decided it was time. Time to share lessons learned from the conversations, the fears, the smiles, the celebrations, the failures, the acceptances, defeats, and the concerns of the many parents I've met along the way. Parents and schools are on this rollercoaster of a journey together, and this book is a cooperative guide to the children's success along the way. There will be many ups and downs, and, in the end, both parents and schools want the same thing for the children: success in school, learning, confidence, engagement, and eventually graduation and the capabilities to enable them to fly independently.

I am a Principal, as well as a parent, and I live both lives. I have had countless interactions with parents and students in my many years as a school leader and have grown into learning what it takes to be successful, in and outside of the classrooms and school building. There are so many tangible and intangible techniques and strategies I share in this book that you can implement in your own household and equip your children with.

As I write this book, my oldest daughter, Claire, is in eighth grade, her third year of middle school; my second child, Matthew, the sixth, first year of middle school; and my youngest, Tessa, in fourth. My wife and I are meeting their teachers, learning the school culture and style, and wanting the best for them. All the while holding our breath, they will be ok knowing we've empowered them to be superstars.

So, we continue the school journey, looking to work closely with our children and teachers to put them in the best position possible.

That is my hope for you and your family after reading this book: bringing *"the partnership"* closer together for the betterment of the child. It is hard to keep your child on the tracks of success--this book is the roadmap for you to help guide your child and build strong, long-lasting relationships with the school community.

In this book, I also share stories from my own childhood that were great lessons in my life. In addition, a number of them derive from my role as Principal, learning from the different experiences of students in my school as well as their parents. Lastly, several families from a variety of backgrounds have also shared with me their stories of things they did for their children to help them along the way. Those stories and more are included in *The Partnership.*

So, again, this book is for you. This book is for me. By reading this book, you will get tips, tricks, and hacks to best interact and work more closely and build relationships with the school for the betterment and success of your child. Your role is to absorb, reflect, and implement the strategies that work for you and your family. Some situations are easy, some can be difficult, but always keep the end goal in mind: for your child to have an enriched and successful school experience while you build and cultivate positive relationships with the school community. #Enjoythejourney

Foreword
By Jay Billy

I am grateful to Jay for his friendship and leadership over the years. Jay is an amazing school leader in New Jersey and author of *Lead with Culture*. He's done so much for many, including writing the forward to this very special project. Love his crazy hats too. Thanks, Jay! #TLAP #LeadLAP Follow him on Twitter @JayBilly2.

I first met Andrew Marotta through his sister Suzanne Carbonaro. I had done some work with Suzanne, and we had talked about her brother, who was a high school principal. Then I had the opportunity to meet Andrew and read his first book, *The Principal Surviving and Thriving* (2nd edition now entitled *The School Leader Surviving & Thriving*), and I knew that this guy gets "it." His book was full of practical and common-sense ideas and practices for principals of any level. Over the last couple of years, since becoming connected with Andrew via social media, we have crossed paths many times, and I always enjoy speaking to him about our schools, our work, and our love for athletics.

Little did I know how much we had in common until Andrew asked me to read this book, his second, *The Partnership Surviving and Thriving*, and then he offered me the honor of writing this foreword.

Although we grew up in different parts of the country, me in Ohio, Andrew in New York, we seem to have many of the same values, which were instilled by our parents and families. In my teenage years, my father used to tell me, as I was going out with friends, "If you do something stupid and get arrested, don't call me until the morning. You know that I'll be sleeping." Luckily, there were many close calls, but no arrests. Like Andrew, athletics was my outlet, and although both my mother and father worked, they supported my involvement and, most of all, always showed up. They not only showed up for all my events, but they were involved and helped in any capacity. They showed the importance of giving back to your community. When severe budget cuts came to our high school and our sports seasons were threatened, my parents, along with many others, started a booster club to make sure that our sports weren't taken from us. They held fund-raising events, ran wrestling tournaments, and filled in wherever they were needed. My father always was on the chain gang during football, while my mother would run the head table at wrestling tournaments. They showed up to every football game and wrestling match I had and then continued the work with the schools, long after I was gone. In fact, both my mother and father are in my High School's Hall of Fame for their dedication and service to the schools. My athletic prowess never even got me close to such awards.

When I went off to college and continued wrestling, my parents continued to show up. No matter where I was competing, they seldom missed a match. They'd work all day and all week, and then they'd show up in some way-out college town to see me wrestle, despite the expense or inconvenience. I probably didn't understand how important "just showing up" was when I was younger, but as I got older, I realized the sacrifices they made. Now, as a father myself, I feel that one of the most important things I can do is be there when my kids need me. Whether it is just to listen, to offer advice, or to give them a hug, being there for your children is the key.

Parenting in the 21st century is a complex and all-encompassing set of skills and decisions that can have a profound effect on the next generation and for generations to come. Each decision we make and action we take as parents either supports our children's growth in a positive way or helps to teach negative behaviors. There is no playbook.

Having said that, as a school principal, we see so many examples of parents who are doing it right and know just when to push, how much to push or just when to sit back and watch. That is what this book is about. It's about the stories of positive parenting that will give you insight into what people are thinking and why. This book gives you perspectives from the parent side of the table and from the educator side of the table. We know that no two situations are alike as we know that no two children are alike. You may not agree with all that is said here, but hopefully, you will see the thoughts and reasoning behind the decisions made. Take what works for you from the stories and situations here and file the rest away for when you need it.

The Pandemic of 2020 is moving quickly into 2021 and has blown the doors off our school buildings. Parents are co-educators right along with the teachers, so we need to be on the same page. *The Partnership: Surviving and Thriving* gives parents and educators examples of how to make the most of this partnership and how to help our kids grow up to be kind, empathetic, responsible, contributing members of their communities. In a world where common sense isn't always so common, this book just makes sense. Enjoy the ride.

—Jay Billy, father, principal, leader and author of *Lead with Culture*

Acknowledgments

I'd like to acknowledge and thank Jennifer, my wife, and my three children, Claire, Matthew, and Tessa. Jenn is an awesome wife, mom, and educator who juggles our household, which gives me time to be me. My children are ages 15, 13, and 10 at the time of publication, and it has been a blessing to be their father. My wife and I are so grateful for our lives growing up and the family life that we have built together in our marriage. Parenting is such a ride with many twists and turns. I thank them for their patience with me, the time they granted me to sit down and actually write this book, and for their forgiveness of me for leaving my stuff around the house! *I'm working on that!* I hope one day they will pass on the stories and lessons from their lives, as well as this book, to their children.

I would also like to thank the friends and family who contributed to this project by sharing their stories, traditions, lessons, techniques, and styles that work in their families: Lynn and John Bell, Genny and Rich Cornell, Denise and Joe Dicks, Haley and David Pulli, Amy and Asael Ruvalcaba, Anna and Al Sackey, Laura and Kevin Spainhour, Bert and Deana Stevenson, and Jenn and Frank Vogel thank you for providing wonderful, meaningful excerpts by sharing aspects of their parenting skills.

A heartfelt thank you to my siblings for their contributions: Suzanne Carbonaro, Maureen Marotta, and Paul Marotta. We had very similar experiences growing up with our parents that left a profound impact on us. Thank you for sharing these impacts in this book. #AlottaMarotta

Additionally, Dr. Rob Gilbert, Sports Psychologist from Montclair State University, has become a great influence on my life and parenting. I have been calling his success hotline 973-743-4690 for years and have learned a tremendous amount. Dr. Rob has become a mentor and friend, and I share many of his messages and lessons throughout this book. His voice echoes in many points of *The Partnership, Surviving and Thriving.* #powerofasingleexperience.

I'd also like to thank my friends Dan Spainhour (Check out his Coaching and Leadership Journal and more at the Leadership Publishing Team.com), Julie Balogh, guidance counselor, Ron Semerano, teacher, and Dan Rockwell, the Leadership Freak, for sharing their stories and writings.

Thanks to the Rickard family for willing to be photographed for the cover and back cover pictures. Born into a family of educators, and now educators themselves, I am grateful to Tom and Amy Rickard and their wonderful children: Thomas, Nicolas, Catherine, and Mary, for being part of this project.

To my friends who helped be part of the focus group for this project: Jennifer Bollinger (my cousin), Omar Brown, Maileen Celis, and Danny Valenzuela.

Lastly, I'd like to thank the many families and students from Port Jervis, NY. We have all grown together over the years through good times and bad, and I thank you for sharing your stories. Also, thanks to Gavin Staerker for being a leader in the front row! Gavin is the class President from the Class of 2019, who you will meet later in the book. An inspiring young man who taught me many things, including the importance of sitting in the front row!

LOVE

L ove, and then a little more. In this chapter, you will find stories and actions of how love can be expressed and received. Notice the variety and types of love, with the message of support. Start with this ingredient, and you can't go wrong.

1. SOMETIMES GO ABOVE AND BEYOND: DAD COMING TO A GAME AT RANDOLPH-MACON COLLEGE.

There are certain things that you remember in your life—some of them almost like they just happened yesterday. There is one memory that I will never forget. I had a great opportunity to play college basketball at Guilford College and be part of the Quaker men's basketball team from 1993 to 1997. I loved every minute of it and felt fortunate and grateful to be on the team. I was not a great athlete but tried really hard. I put my heart and soul into it and again loved being a fighting Quaker. I was 10 hours from Staten Island where I grew up, so there were definitely times during my playing career that I was quite homesick. We were the most southern school in an all Virginia conference, and we were located in Greensboro, North Carolina. So our closest road trip was two hours in the Old Dominion Athletic Conference, ODAC.

In my junior year, we had some new players on the team that had beat me out for playing time, and I was not playing much. There were trips where we would ride the bus for five hours to play the game and five hours back, and I would never get off the bench. Those were long days, and little did I know that those days on the bench would help me in my officiating career later in life, but that's another story for another day. This particular story takes place in Randolph Macon, Virginia. The Quakers were playing a weekday game against the Yellow Jackets at 7 p.m., and Randolph Macon College is located approximately seven hours from Staten Island, New York. It was midway through the first half when I thought I saw my dad sitting up in the stands. I did a double-take and couldn't believe it was my dad! I stood up and actually waved to him from the bench, and he waved back. Going into halftime, I ran up and gave him a quick hug, and came back. I was so excited for him to be there, and my hopes to play certainly increased.

Well, it went on to be a tight game, which we wound up losing only by a few points, so I never left the bench. While I was disappointed we lost, I was further disappointed that I didn't get in the game. I was actually embarrassed that my dad had driven the whole way, and I didn't get off the bench. After showers, which I really didn't need, I had a few minutes to talk with him before we boarded the bus. He said hello to some of my friends and shook my coach's hand, who thanked my dad for attending the game. I got a little teary-eyed and actually said I was sorry I didn't get to play. He looked at me as he always did and put his two big hands around my cheeks, and said, "Andrew, I didn't care if you played or not. I came to be with you and support you. You'll understand one day." I'm actually crying while writing this right now because of what that meant to me.

He drove 14 hours from and back to New York just to see me, got home at 4 o'clock in the morning, then went to work. I'll never forget that story, and I share it with you because sometimes you have to go above and beyond. Sometimes you have to do the extraordinary for your kids. Those are the moments that they will remember forever. My mom and dad always loved me and always treated me well, but these moments of extraordinary love and dedication are the ones I remember so fondly. While I was embarrassed and upset at the moment, I am so grateful for that memory. There were so many other such times, but this one stands out in my memory because I never asked, nor expected, him to be there. He just drove on a whim to watch a game during which I didn't even get off the bench! Both my mom and dad were there for me so many times. If you have a chance to do something extraordinary with or for your child, do it. They will remember it forever.

2. THIS IS A MARATHON, NOT A SPRINT.

26.2 miles. Yes. It is a marathon, yet we are not talking about running here. We are talking and sharing about the educational process and the life of your child. This is a long journey. There are going to be (or there have been if you are a veteran parent!) a lot of ups and downs. Your child will excel in certain areas and fall in others. This is OK. We are human, and we are going to make mistakes. I laugh now thinking back to when I was a kid growing up in the '70s and '80s.

Our parents just let us be. We were out all day, every day, and they didn't know where...we just were. Drinking from the water hose, riding our bikes all over with no helmet, and NO CELL PHONES. I feel so old writing these things, yet it amazes me. So, take a deep breath, and let your child be. As my good friend and teacher, Ilene Valentin, says, "They only get one childhood." Let them run the race, but know that it is a long journey." It is a marathon, not a sprint—a marathon full of love, amazing times, and unforgettable memories. Love them throughout. Enjoy the race, keep them running, and every once in a while, they will have to stop to tie their shoe, stop at the medical tent, stretch, eat, and maybe take a break. #Keeprunning! #Keeploving

3. RICH OR POOR—IT DOESN'T MATTER.

The following is shared from Dan Spainhour's book, *Leading Narratives*, which is a great collection of stories and lessons:

One day a father of a very wealthy family took his son on a trip to the country with a firm purpose of showing his son what poverty looks like. They spent a couple of days and nights on the farm of what would be considered a very poor family. On their return from the trip, the father asked his son how the trip was.

"It was great, Dad!" his son replied.

"Did you see how poor people can be?" the father asked.

"Oh yeah," stated the son.

"So what did you learn from the trip?" The father continued.

His son replied, "I saw we have one dog, and they have four. We have a pool that reaches to the middle of the garden, and they have a creek that has no end. We have imported lanterns in our garden, and they have stars at night. Our patio reaches to the front yard, and they have a whole horizon. We have a small piece of land to live on, but they have fields that go beyond our sight. We have servants who serve us, but they serve others. We buy our food, but they grow theirs. We have walls around our property that protect us. They have friends to protect them."

With this, the boy's father was speechless. Then his son added: "Thanks, Dad, for showing me how poor we are."

Everything is about perspective, and your perspective may not be the same as those you are trying to influence. Thanks to Dan Spainhour for sharing this great story.

4. SEE WHAT CAN HAPPEN WHEN YOU OPEN YOUR DOOR. MEET DAVE PULLI.

See what can happen: LOVE Happens when you open your doors and home for others. This excerpt is written by Dave Pulli: brother, friend, son.

In 1999, I moved to New York State to spend a year volunteering in a program run by the Order of Saint Augustine located in a church on Staten Island. While volunteering, I was fortunate to work with Andrew Marotta. We became friends and roommates. At the end of that year, I decided to stay in New York and pursue a graduate degree in Social Work, and Andrew had decided to pursue opportunities in Italy. In turn, my finances and living situation shifted. Unbeknownst to me, Andrew spoke with his parents (Joe [Mr. Joe] and Dore Marotta), and he asked if they would be open to having me stay with them while he was away. Although I don't know the exact conversation, I imagine that it was an interesting exchange.

At that time, Dore and Mr. Joe had four adult children and three grandchildren. Why would they consider taking a twenty-something-year-old man beginning graduate school into their home? I can't say how open I would have been. However, they not only welcomed me into their home, they made it clear to me that I was not to be just a tenant, but a part of the family, no negotiations. Their willingness to invite me into their lives speaks tremendously to who they are as individuals and parents. Although I was well beyond my formidable developing years, Mr. Joe and Dore showed me love, support, and care as if I were their own son. I don't think that they expected me to stay as long as I did (seven years), and I certainly didn't expect to gain an extended family.

As the years flew by, I had the chance to watch them with their children and grandchildren, and I was lucky enough to be a part of many family milestone events: the good times and the not so good times. Through it all, I saw Dore and Mr. Joe provide the love and guidance that I believe are pivotal to being a parent. As a relatively new father myself, I often find myself questioning my actions and reevaluating what I am doing. I tend to reflect upon my own experiences with my parents in Boston, and tethered to that, my life with Mr. Joe and Dore. When I'm thinking about my time with the Marottas, it often circles back to three main aspects: love, being available, and self-reflection.

They were willing to open their hearts and share their love of family with me. It was at numerous family gatherings that I witnessed them being at their happiest. It didn't matter the occasion, as long as we were all there. It was also in the quiet moments, sharing a meal together or watching a favorite TV show. We would discuss the current state of affairs with the family. Most often, it would revolve around how to help in one circumstance or another. This taught me that being a parent is an ongoing journey. It doesn't stop as soon as the kids are grown and out of the house. Their many examples of love help to remind me to keep my heart open to my family, but also to others in my life. It also reminds me to enjoy having my family together on as many occasions as possible.

I am also made aware of the way Dore and Mr. Joe made themselves available for their family. They would balance their lives so that they could be accessible and present for their children. Thinking about their dedication to this facet of parenthood helps me see what I need to do to be there for my children and my wife. It reminds me that family is what is most important. When I consider self-reflection, I think about some of my conversations with Mr. Joe. We talked about his children often, and sometimes he would reminisce about the past. He would pause frequently and make comments like, "Maybe I was too strict," or "I could have done that differently." I can't speak to any particular situation and how it was handled, but his comments have been a consistent reminder to me to think about how I am doing as a father and husband. Do I need to consider different approaches or look to improve what I am doing?

Ultimately, ensuring that I love enough, make myself available, and reflect often not only applies to being a parent, but they're great lessons for living a full life. Thank you, Dore and Mr. Joe.

—*Dave Pulli*

Little loving eyes
There are little eyes upon you,
they are watching you night and day,
there are little ears that quickly
Take in every word you say.
You're the little one's idol,
you're the wisest of the wise
and in his or her little mind about you,
no suspicions ever rise.
You are setting an example
Every day in all you do;
for the little child who's waiting,
to grow up to be just like you.

Unknown author

5. LOVE 'EM WITH ALL YOUR HEART BY JOHN BELL

Written by Dr. John Bell, father, husband, mentor, and Superintendent of Delaware Valley Schools, Milford, PA

I've had a lot of great jobs over the years, but nothing compares to being a parent! It can be an awesome, rewarding experience with tons of love and pride. It can also be demanding, frustrating, and a lot of hard work. There is an old saying that "the days can be long (especially when the kids are little), but the years go fast." It is so true.

Lynne and I always enforced a rule with our boys that both of us had when we were growing up in the 1970s: "If you get in trouble in school, you will get it twice as bad at home." It might seem old-fashioned, but you aren't doing your kids any favors when you race to the school to defend them every time they have an issue. Helicopter parents want the best for their kids, as we all do, but they don't realize that part of growing up is to become more independent and responsible for your own actions. Sometimes you have to let them fail and figure out a way to bounce back. I can tell you from experience that it can get messy, but it's part of the maturation process.

When our boys reached middle school age, they started asking about going to other kids' houses to visit and/or sleepover. Our rule was that they couldn't go to someone's house that we didn't know, and we had to confirm that the parents would be there to supervise.

As they got older and moved from middle school to high school and eventually college, the school work got harder. This is where we had to coach and guide them more than tell them any particular course of action. We wanted them to figure out their options and what the pros and cons of each option were. This is a skill that they can use throughout their adult lives – accepting a job, buying a house, and selecting a spouse are just a few of the big decisions they will face.

In closing, I would say to love them with all your heart, support them in all of their activities, and set and enforce reasonable rules. They won't be perfect, nor will you, but they will grow to love and respect you more and more as the years go by. —*Dr. John Bell*

6. IN THIS FAMILY, LOVE IS SPELLED TIME.

This is what kids really want. In a day and age where parents are busier than ever, and cell phones and apps have infiltrated our lives, kids want time. "Unfiltered, undistracted time." I read this quote somewhere, and my wife and I decided to put it on a plaque in our home. Our family, like many others, is very busy—soccer, musicals, family obligations, trips, babysitting, etc. These are all positive and important family times together, but they pull us in different directions away from being home just having quiet time. As I write this, it is a rainy fall Sunday, and all activities are canceled. After church, we are all home together, cooking, doing homework, exercising, and maybe even working in a nap. It's a nice calm day even though the weather outside is not pleasant...

I'm looking forward to an evening of family fun watching the Food Network Halloween cooking competitions, Halloween Wars. The night before, we carved our own pumpkins together, which we proudly displayed on our mantle with candles illuminating the scary faces.

7. PAUL, DAD, AND THE STORY OF THE KIDNEY

How do you set up the scenario so that you take care of your children when they need you, and then your children will take care of you when you need them? I watched this happen in front of my eyes as my Dad's diabetes grew worse and his health continued to fail. My whole life, I watched my mother and father suffer through the ups and downs of him having diabetes. It is a terrible disease, especially for someone who liked to eat and probably cheated on food choices too many times, and it began to negatively affect his kidney function. This was in the year 2004. My father was initially resistant to the idea of one of us donating a kidney, yet eventually, he relented. He saw the writing on the wall and did not want to go down the avenue of dialysis. Well, there we were, seven of us going to get tested to see if any of us would be a match. My three brothers, my mom, my father's sister (Aunt Maryann), our pseudo-adopted brother Dave Pulli, and I were all hoping to be the one that would be able to donate a kidney to this amazing man. The nurses at the kidney unit at Columbia Presbyterian said they had never seen so many people volunteering to donate for one person. We kind of looked at each other and shrugged our shoulders and said, well, of course, we would. That was a defining moment when I told myself that I wanted to live my life as my mom and dad did by constantly giving of themselves to us for the betterment of our lives and our families. They were selfless and always put our family first no matter what. My brother Paul stepped up to be the kidney donor as the oldest male in the family as well as his massive size! This made for a good kidney match and eventually a successful surgery. He was adamant about this decision, and while I wanted to help my Pops, I admired Paul's courage and resolve.

I watched Paul's and my father's lives change immensely, and the two of them grew even closer. It was a beautiful story to watch: a son and father sharing with one another. This procedure enriched both my mom's and Dad's lives, and I am eternally grateful to my brother for the sacrifice he made for Dad.

Live your life and care for your children so as to create an environment that they will do the same for you when the time comes.

8. SERVICE TO OTHERS

Serving others with your children is one of the best things you can do. It teaches you and them so many things. It shows children about empathy, kindness, and the unfortunate economic diversity that exists in our world. While it is nice to donate money to causes and put a check in the basket each week at church, doing actual service with your children for others will bring you closer. Some examples could be going to the local food pantry or animal shelter, working with Habitat for Humanity, or even just raking the leaves in a neighbor's yard. These actions will not only model social responsibility, but also strengthen the bonds of mutual respect between you and your child. My parents and in-laws modeled this for me, especially Joe Marotta, my Dad, and Eugene Grimes, my father-in-law, who has truly been a second father to me. My father started the food pantry in our church in Staten Island, New York, along with his sister, my mother, and several other close friends. They began serving the community members of Tompkinsville on the North Shore of Staten Island near the ferry. My parents would bring my siblings and me along each Saturday morning. We helped stock the shelves, pack the bags, and distribute the food to the needy. We were always running around the city picking up food and items to give away. One time we even went to Yankee Stadium to get extra giveaways that they had from a game. Here I am now, 30 years later, doing the same with my kids, all because of that experience. Second, my children are watching their grandfather, Eugene Grimes, dedicate his time and talent to Habitat for Humanity. Eugene has always been helping others his whole life by building and fixing things for everyone and everybody. If something was to be done, Eugene Grimes was there to do it. Since his retirement, he has been active in Habitat for Humanity and has built several homes and worked on numerous projects serving our community in northeast Pennsylvania. He truly is a role model. The point of highlighting my fathers is to stress how important it is to model service to others for your children so in their lives they will do the same.

9. VOICE BY ANNA SACKEY

Anna Sackey and her husband Al are the parents of Konotey, Korkor, and Lartiokor. Konotey was diagnosed with autism at the age of 2 and is now a happy, thriving teenager. Anna, an elementary school teacher, authored a guidebook for families with children newly diagnosed with autism. More information on this book and her blog can be found on her website breathoffaith.com.

We are our children's voice and strongest advocates. Even though my husband and I were both educators and had earned multiple graduate degrees in education, it took becoming parents of a special needs child for us to truly understand that we are our children's voice, and it's up to us to speak up for them and advocate for what they need.

When our son was diagnosed with autism, it felt I was hit by a truck, and our world was smashed into a million pieces--mine and his. I quickly realized that it was up to me to educate and empower myself to learn all I could about what I could do to help him. I became equipped and empowered because not only did I educate myself about his diagnosis, but more importantly, as his mom, I knew him better than anyone, and I found I could educate his providers on him specifically. I could help them understand *my* child and what he needed.

Over the years since, my husband and I have attended countless IEP and 504 meetings for all three of our children, who have all struggled with and overcome a variety of challenges. For every meeting, we've learned to go in with a list of exactly how we think they are doing, what is going well, what they are struggling with, and what exactly we would like as an outcome of the meeting. We go in with an attitude of warmth and collaboration, prepared with an idea of exactly what we would like, and of course, we say a prayer right beforehand.

I couldn't be more proud of my children. All children are different, and all children are beautiful. Yes, we each have struggles that we go through in life, but we all just need some support, tweaks, and shifts that will help us on our way. Our job as parents is to nurture our children, to guide them, and to be their defenders and advocates in this world. And one of the ways we do that is by being our children's voice, as we work on helping them develop and strengthen their own unique voice to speak up for themselves and on behalf of others.

—*Anna Sackey*

10. PROTECT YOUR CHILDREN: SHOW ME THAT BOY!

The year was 1990, and my sister Maureen was a sophomore at the University of Cortland in upstate New York. She was already homesick and not thrilled with being away from home, but my parents made her stay up there to continue her studies. She attended a semi-formal dance on a Saturday night. On Sunday afternoon, Maureen called home to my mother and father, crying on the phone, upset that people were talking about her. She went with a young man to the event that she knew casually, and that boy was spreading rumors about things they had done together the evening before. These rumors were untrue, and Maureen was devastated. She felt attacked, lonely, and betrayed that people were saying and thinking these things of her. As she vented to my parents, they listened and tried their best to comfort her over the phone.

The next morning Maureen had a knock at the door around 8 a.m. It was my father. Shocked and startled, Maureen asked what he was doing here. He responded in a firm voice with the now infamous words, "Show me that boy!" Nervously, Maureen walked my dad to the cafeteria in search of the young man with whom she attended the semi-formal. They entered the cafeteria together, and Maureen pointed to the far end of the cafeteria, where the boy sat eating with some of his friends. My father kissed her on the cheek, hugged her, said everything will be OK, and walked off towards the young man. Maureen watched in astonishment as my father walked over, shook the young man's hand, and began speaking with him. Minutes later, my dad and sister walked out of the cafeteria together. Maureen did not know what to think. Later that afternoon, Maureen saw the boy during dinner time, and he apologized in front of a number of people and went on his way. This put an end to the rumors, and Maureen's spirits were uplifted. She never heard from the boy again, nor did she have any further problems with that situation.

So what is the takeaway from the story? Protect your children. Be fearless. Throughout this book, there are so many different scenarios in which you have to make judgment calls. In other tips, I talk about letting your children figure it out on their own. Be mindful of not interfering or being a helicopter parent. These are judgment calls for you and your spouse to make for each and every situation. In this scenario, my mother and father felt it best to get involved. My dad woke up at 4 a.m. that morning to drive to upstate New York to be there at breakfast time. I would love to know what was said in that conversation, but I will never know. What I do know is that it fixed the situation and comforted my sister during a time when she needed it. Teenagers, even older teenagers, can be fragile as their bodies and minds are still developing. So even though they may be tough and gruff on the outside, they still need their parents, as my sister in this situation needed her parents to ensure the restoration of her reputation. My father drove back to Staten Island to be at work by lunchtime. Just another day at the office for my mom and dad as parents, yet something that my family remembers forever.

I never knew the story until my dad's passing when we sat around the dining room table sharing stories of all the things that my mom and dad had done for us. I was truly amazed by this one and still am today. I have two young daughters, as well as a son, for whom I am ready to take action if the need arises. Take this story and stick it in your pocket and be ready to act when the time comes for you.

11. THE MOST DIFFICULT JOB IN THE WORLD BY ASAEL RUVALCABA

Asael Ruvalcaba, also known as "Mr. R," is an energized, progressive Principal in South Texas. He leads the #Sendit crew at school and for his family. He is active on Twitter @Asael_Ruvalcaba.

Parenting, by far, is the most difficult job in the world! I always try to start any parent assembly with that statement. I want parents to know *that I know* that parenting is not easy and that I need them as much as they need us. I believe a partnership and a team approach between home and school must exist. In addition, I share that there are three things that parents can do to make their child successful in school and life.

I always recommend to parents that they should assign house chores to their children. I understand many parents just want their children to focus on school work, but it has been shown that if children have responsibilities and duties around the house, they will grow up to be responsible adults.

Another big thing is to tell your children that you love them every single day. Too often, I see students acting out to seek attention. Many of them crave love because they are not receiving the love and attention at home. Children need to hear this four-lettered word from their mom, dad, or guardian daily. Trust me, a simple text with an "I Love You" will have a lasting impact.

My last advice to parents is to ensure that their child sees them as the parent and not a friend. There has to be some respect for authority. For me personally, the last words I want to hear from a teacher or principal were... "I will be calling your parents." There have been numerous times when I tell this to students, and there is no fear, nor do I get a reaction from them. Instantly, I know that there are larger issues at home.

Amy and I are not the perfect parents by any means, and we do not have all the answers. We both come from different backgrounds and experiences, but at the end of the day, we make it work for our five children, Annika, Clarissa, April, Briana, and AJ. Parenting is definitely challenging. We believe in these practices: house chores should be a given, tell your children that you love them, ensure that you act as a parent and not a friend, and trust that your children will be better students. I am happy and proud to pass them on from our family to yours.

—Asael Ruvalcaba

STUDENT LIFE

"*How can I possibly be expected to handle school on a day like this?*"

— *FERRIS BUELLER FROM THE CLASSIC MOVIE FERRIS BUELLER'S DAY OFF*

We want more than just "handling" school. We want more than just surviving. Work with your child to implement these tips in this chapter to help build successful habits while in school, unlike Ferris Bueller and his day off!

13. THERE ARE NO BAD KIDS—JUST KIDS THAT MAKE POOR DECISIONS OR BEHAVE BADLY AT TIMES.

There's a country music song by Luke Bryant entitled, "Most People are Good." I believe that, and I believe in the goodness of others. When their children are born, all parents want them to do great things during their lives. And most parents follow through on their work as parents.

As a high school principal, I have seen many students go astray, and I believe the number one factor is a lack of structure, routines, and commitment to the school in their early years in the family setting as a whole. I have never blamed parents nor do I judge them because they are each doing the best that they know how. Sometimes, from the perspective of an outsider looking in, it may look like a simple decision or an easy fix; however, when it's your life and your world, it may not be so easy.

I don't believe there are any bad kids out there. Unfortunately, some young people have been left to their own devices; they have not been appropriately corrected when they have done wrong or made unwise decisions. They don't have the support needed to correct these behaviors. It upsets me each time a young person is arrested for drugs (whether it's using or selling), and then we find out that the parent was also involved in helping sell or distribute the drugs. That one hurts.

If you believe that you can help each kid and believe that there is goodness in them, the hope of correcting those mistakes in their behaviors is always better. If you have a moment, listen to the words of that song, "Most People are Good." Most kids are good, too. Somewhere along their journeys, they might have lacked guidance and now must be offered helpful interventions to adjust their decision-making skills.

14. SIT IN THE FRONT ROW: ASK GAVIN STAERKER.

I did an activity in the 2018-2019 school year as principal in which I shadowed our senior class president. He was an ambitious, intelligent young man eager in so many areas of his life. I admired his enthusiasm for learning and school spirit. It was a fascinating day learning so much being in all his classes and experiencing the student's perspective all day. By the third period, I noticed something unique about Gavin. He was sitting in the front row in every class. He would get to the class, take out his books and work ready to get started again. By mid-day, I asked him about this, and he said, "Oh, that's easy. You get so much more in the front row. You can learn more because you are closer to the action." This was very telling about this young man. His chin was always up, eyes focused, and dialed in. I know this is for many reasons, yet one big one, according to Gavin, was sitting in the front row. There are only a few seats up in the front, and rarely do people sit upfront. Challenge your child to do so. Leaders lead the way. I know I learned a lot more during this day than Gavin did! Thank you Gavin!

15. DON'T JUST ASK YOUR KID: HOW WAS SCHOOL TODAY?

Try asking your child, "What is one thing you learned today," "What is one thing you liked about school today," or "What was one thing you did not like?" I learned this conversation tip from a teacher and mom at Port Jervis High School. In our conversation, she explained that these questions generate conversations with your kids. Most times, when you ask a child, "How was school today?" they're going to say fine. Great. It was OK. But more pointed, targeted questions will generate follow-up conversations between you and your child. You can ask additional questions like, "Why did you like that?" or "

How did it make you feel?" Questions like these will enable you to dig more deeply into your child's journey in school and discover, overall, how they're doing. You will begin to learn their likes and dislikes as well as the habits of their teachers and friends. Give it a try. I think you will be happy with the results.

If we continue to ask the same questions, we are going to get the same answers. By asking questions that require thoughtfully evaluated responses, you spark your child's curiosity. Often students may have questions, but they are afraid to be the ones to stick their hand in the air. Whether it is because they are more curious about aspects of the subject or they did not really understand the concept, kids are afraid to ask questions. If you challenge your kid daily to ask questions during classes, that will help break down the fear knowing that mom and dad think it's OK to ask questions. Try to model these behaviors whenever a learning moment presents itself. When you find yourself with your child in an aquarium, museum, or some sort of presentation, if you ask questions, you are modeling the behavior that you expect. If they do not have an immediate answer, give them some time to consider a response and then ask, "Well, now that you've had a chance to think about it, do you have any questions for me that might help you come up with an answer?"

These types of conversations with your child will only boost their confidence to be able to ask the right questions, but also build up their conversational skills when sharing their school day with you in detail. Try it. I bet you will be glad you did.

16. STANDARDIZED TESTS

Do not get caught up in the anxiety of standardized tests. Instead, buy into the famous saying from WWII and the spirit of Winston Churchill: Keep calm and carry-on. Well, keep calm and have your kid take the standardized test. Some people lose their minds over these things, and your child will have these tests from kindergarten through twelfth grade. Yes, including getting into college, the famous SAT!

Just tell them to be calm, do their best, and not stress out. Certainly, you can make sure they go to bed on time, that they have a nourishing breakfast, and are prepared with pencils, pens, and a bottle of water. I know there are also districts and testing situations that don't even allow water. The point is rules and procedures must be followed, so don't get caught up in the hype and hysteria of these exams.

Sometimes there may even be over concern by the teacher because many teacher evaluations may depend on the results. This is the job of the leadership team at the school as well as teachers themselves to remain calm. Set the environment for kids to be successful. If the adults stay calm and focused on what the point is, then so too will the children. In the end, as I wrote in tip number 38, the results are not the end all be all. I know plenty of students who maybe did not perform as well on standardized tests yet made up for it in other areas. My sister Suzanne (featured in tip number 72) scored below expectations on her first SAT attempt. She had a B+ average in college prep in high school. Suzanne wound up graduating magna cum laude from Plattsburgh University in NY and attained two master's degrees from elite institutions. In the end, the tests may seem important in the moment yet, in the big picture, your children will get to where they need to be. Suzanne is a great example of this.

In short, yes, these tests can be important, but they are not the end all be all. It is NOT "this is it, it's do or die, it's now or never, this is my only shot!" Test anxiety or worry will hinder your child's performance, not help it. Encourage your child to do their best, and that's it.

Too much pressure is too much pressure. *#Don'tSweatIt. #KeepCalmAndTestOn!*

17. VISIT INTERNATIONALLY DURING THEIR SCHOOLING.

If finances allow, consider international travel. This is something that my wife and I did soon after our college graduation. I highly recommend this for you, and we are going to do this for our own children when they turn 16. During my senior year, after graduating from Guilford College, I had an opportunity to go backpacking across Europe with several of my college buddies. #TripOfALifetime We had an amazing experience drinking wine in the hills of Tuscany, renting a house in the south of France, having fish and chips in England, and seeing all the amazing sites in Germany and beyond.

This whet my appetite to experience more of Europe, and when we got engaged, my wife expressed she wanted to have some amazing experiences before we settled down with jobs and children. We discussed several different options, including the Peace Corps, Teach for America, and others. Right around this time, our family priest, Father Joe Mostardi, OSA, was leaving our parish, the Roman Catholic Church of Our Lady of Good Counsel in St. George Staten Island, to start Augustinian Volunteers. This is a service-based volunteer program based out of Villanova University and the Order of Augustinians.

After some back-and-forth discussions with our family, the Augustinians, and one another, we decided to go for it. We were the guinea pigs as the program was only in its experimental first year. I went and lived in a monastery, the church of Sant Agostino, in San Gimignano, Italy, in the Tuscany region between Siena and Florence. Jennifer, my fiancée at the time, went to London, England, and lived in an existing volunteer program through the Augustinians. We had a chance to visit one another; I went to England and Ireland with Jennifer, and she came back to Italy with me. We celebrated New Year's Eve, 1999, in Saint Peter's Square, enjoyed long walks on the Cliffs of Moher, warm shepherd's pie in the pubs of England, and shared so many other learning experiences that could fill another whole book.

We loved it and want to whet the same appetite for adventure in our children. At the age of 16, we will allow each child to spin the globe and select wherever he/she would like to go and make a family trip out of it. Just talking and planning the trips will be exciting for the whole family. Certainly, we know there will be an expense, and we are budgeting as we go. Being abroad and making international travel part of your child's educational experience, whether through the school or not, can add a lot of value to their lives and enrich their education.

There will be so many opportunities, whether it is a class trip, a trip through one of the school departments, or something on your own like I described. Take advantage of these opportunities and let your kids go. What is the old saying? "Give your children wings so one day they can fly!"

You may be thinking, how can I afford this? How can I manage this with my family circumstance as it is? I would say: do the best you can, as in all things. If travel internationally is not financially possible for you and your family, are there other opportunities for your child? Are there scholarships available? Is there something you could trade out in exchange for the opportunity for a trip? Is there a national trip they could go on instead?

At my high school where I am Principal, Port Jervis High School, some cannot afford the senior trip outright. What can be done? They fundraise, they earn shares through time in the concession stand at home football games, they ask grandma and grandpa to donate or give their birthday money early. We are also blessed with a number of generous staff and alumni who make donations, creating special memories for kids.

I remember my senior year of college, there was no spring break, no holiday break, yet long days and long hours of odd jobs to save money for my graduation trip. My folks told me if I did not have the money, I wasn't going, so I scrapped it all together, including borrowing money from my buddies' folks to be able to go (#grateful).

These opportunities can be a financial strain. The point is, where, and whenever possible, try to create opportunities for them to travel. These experiences can change a youngster's life.

18. THERE MAY BE MERIT TO HAVING YOUR KIDS WORK THROUGH A CLASS THEY DO NOT LIKE OR STAY WITH A TEACHER OF WHOM THEY ARE NOT FOND.

A call I receive as Principal several times a year is parents requesting a change in placement for their child in the teacher's class. Whether there is a personality conflict, the kid does not like the class, or specifically, they are complaining about the teacher, I get this request multiple times a year. I always facilitate a conversation between the parent and the teacher along with the student. Maybe it is something simple that is an easy fix on our end, and sometimes the teacher makes a slight adjustment, and all is well. Sometimes I do change the class depending on the circumstances.

The conversation that I do have with the parents is advising them to have their children work through their issues. I certainly speak with the staff if it is a specific something that they might be doing that is upsetting this student, or are they embarrassing the student unintentionally, but I do feel it is important for students to work through difficult times. I tell parents that they are going to have bosses they don't like, coaches they don't like, and situations in life where they don't like the person yet they have to deal with it. If we make every accommodation to make the student happy and comfortable, where is the struggle? Where is the, "I have to suck it up and just do what I have to do in this situation?"

So many successful people in life are successful because they are persistent, relentless, and resilient. We all have hurdles and issues in life that we must work through, and this is a learning opportunity for students. So I caution parents before they rush in to see the principal to take some time to carefully analyze the circumstances with their child. Give your child some tools and techniques they can use to work through situations when they might not like a class or a particular teacher. There will be an end to this time, and, just as in real life, sometimes we must deal with the circumstances and situations around us just as they are because that's a living reality.

19. TAKE ACTION: "YOUR THOUGHTS DETERMINE WHAT YOU WANT, YOUR ACTIONS DETERMINE WHAT YOU GET."

I love the quote to open this tip about taking action from my friend Dr. Rob Gilbert. Dr. Rob is a sports psychologist from Montclair St. University. It leads me to the story of the candle. I was recently at a leadership workshop where we met a fantastic presenter. He was inspirational and motivational, and he ended with a story. He took out a candle and held it in front of us. He lit it and said, "We are going to work together to put this candle out. I want everyone to close your eyes, and let's wish this candle out." So the room of a hundred people closed their eyes, and I saw a bunch of scrunched faces as if people were trying to do something. He said, "Open your eyes," and of course, we still saw a burning candle. Then he commented, "Okay, that didn't work. We are going to chant this candle out." So, once again, the group of a hundred people started to chant, "Out, out, out!"

I felt silly and questioned myself, "What exactly is he trying to get at?" He then made a sarcastic face, looked at us, and said, "What's wrong with you?" He licked his thumb and forefinger and extinguished the candle between them. His point? If you want things to happen, you must take action!

Your children are going to have hopes and dreams, and one of your many jobs is to help facilitate these hopes and dreams into reality. Urge them to take action. They will make mistakes along the way, and you can't save everything. Some of the greatest lessons I've learned along the way were through loss: when I lost my wallet, when I lost my gym shorts, or when I lost the directions to where I was going. All of these were learning opportunities. If your children make a mistake along the way on their journey, it will only make them better. You help them make a plan, help them get started, and then urge them to action.

One great example I think of about taking action is a story from Bruce Springsteen's book called *Springsteen*. I love this story Bruce shares in the book, in his early years of getting started in music. His band drove to California to try to get some gigs. After playing a few small shows, they got an opportunity to try out for a big venue. They did their set and wound up not getting selected. They were devastated.

With not much money or confidence, Bruce and the band packed up and headed back to New Jersey with two junkie cars and a small trailer. It was the middle of winter, and one of the cars broke down in the midwest on Interstate 80. They were broke and really had no options. They decided to junk the car, yet they did not have enough room to fit everyone in just one car. Bruce drew the small straw and had to lay in the back of a closed trailer in the middle of winter closed in, like being a coffin doing 70 mph down the highway. Bruce was terrified as well as devastated, but he did it, and they took turns for two hours at a time riding East. At that moment, as Bruce lay in the dark with his eyes closed, he said to himself he would never NOT get the gig again. This was his 'call to action' moment. He would outwork, outwrite, and out-create other artists to make sure that something like this did not happen again. How did that work out for him? If his parents sent a rental car, maybe we never even know who Bruce Springsteen is.

20. THERE IS NO PRICE TAG ON YOUR CHILD'S EDUCATION.

My mom and dad used to say this all the time. I understand that we're all coming from different backgrounds and financial circumstances. True, people's concerns are valid about the price tag of education. I chose to put this quote in the book, though, because I do believe you get what you pay for. In the long run, investing in your child's education is going to pay off. Whether it is tutoring, college, private school, or extra credit resources, investing in your child's education is a worthwhile investment. When you look back when it is all said and done, which will you say? *I'm glad I did, or I wish I had?*

This brings up two stories to share. The first story is about my mother's experience at St. John's University in the 1960s. My mom was in her second year and was unable to pay the tuition in the fall of her second year. She went to the Financial Aid Office and sat down with the secretary and told her she would have to withdraw because her parents could not afford the tuition that year. The secretary went into the back and got one of the nuns who was working in the office. The Vincentian nun called my mom into the back office.

She asked my mom about her family situation and why she couldn't stay. My mom shared her story that she needed to get home to work and help support the family. The nun took my mom's hand and, looking her in the eye, said, " Dorothy, we want you to remain at St. John's. Don't worry about the tuition for this semester. Come

February, your family should be prepared to pay, but at this time, we will waive your tuition for this semester. When you have the money in the future, you can repay your debt."

My mother was thrilled and completed her studies at St. John's, where she met my dad. She went on to a career in medical technology and has always loved Saint John's. She and my dad have probably donated back that tuition money tenfold.

The second story was my own decision concerning college. I was a senior at Xaverian High School in Bay Ridge, Brooklyn. I really wanted to play college basketball, and I was doing most of the promoting myself. It came down to Guilford College in Greensboro, North Carolina, and Western Maryland. I remember going back and forth on the phone with the Financial Aid offices concerning the expenses, and it came down to a difference of several thousand dollars. There are many ways to advocate for funding while working with the Financial Aid office. One of the best is consistent and persistent communication and being your biggest advocate of why they should offer you more money.

I also weighed the distance away from home and the opportunity I would actually have to play. In the end, it wasn't necessarily the money that determined the final decision, but many factors, including the distance. In retrospect, I believe it was the right choice. I certainly will never know what my experience would've been like at Western Maryland, yet I had to jump in this experience at Guilford and would not trade any of it.

Point of the stories? It's not always about the money. Certainly, when you're digging in your pocket, and there's nothing there to pay the bill, I get it; however, try to look at the big picture. Try to look at it, as I've said many times in this book, as the process and not the end result. Will that school experience make your child a better person and create opportunities to grow into the person you have been training all these years?

Exhaust all your options. Get to know that financial aid officer inside and out. Talk about loans. Talk to a financial expert early and often about the best ways to pay for college. Start saving early, including opening a college account right away. Investing $25 a paycheck adds up over 18 years! All these and more are ways to get started and find solutions for a giant task.

These financial and school selection decisions are for you and your family to make together, but keep in the back of your mind my dad's words: "There is no price tag on your child's education."

21. HOW CAN YOUR CHILD'S MOST DIFFICULT CHALLENGE BECOME A POSITIVE?

The story of Leo and his one arm

Leo was born with one arm. He never really knew any different as a youngster and had a happy childhood. As he grew into middle school age, his parents wanted to toughen him up and asked Leo if he would like to get involved with wrestling. Leo was a little hesitant but a happy-go-lucky kid and said, "Sure, I'll try it." He went to the first dojo with his parents, and the instructor looked at Leo and said, "I'm sorry. He only has one arm. What can I teach him? He will get destroyed in the competition."

Leo's parents quickly ushered their son out of the dojo. Another dojo and a similar result followed. But they were determined and went to the third dojo where instructor Jones looked at Leo and said, "Sure! Suit up, kid." They outfitted Leo in a mixed martial art uniform and began training. Leo and Coach Jones bonded, as they practiced one move day after day. Leo began to get very good at the one move and wondered why he wasn't learning any other moves.

One day he asked Coach Jones if he could learn another move.

Coach Jones calmly nodded no and said, "We are going to continue to practice this one move." After a couple more months of training, Leo began to get a little bored with just the one move. When Coach Jones said it was time for a competition, Leo and his parents were a bit concerned. How could he compete with other kids with two arms, and he only knew one move?

Coach Jones nodded calmly again and said, "Don't worry. Leo is doing just fine." The next weekend Leo went to his first competition with only his left arm, and his empty shirt sleeve tucked behind him. Leo began his first competition. The other opponent did not really know how to approach Leo, so he went in for a quick pin, and Leo quickly took the other boy down and pinned him. Leo was stunned, as were his parents. Coach Jones smiled and was ready to move onto the next opponent.

The next match produced a similar outcome, and before long, it was later in the afternoon and Leo was in the finals of his first tournament. The other boy was very athletic and determined to beat Leo even though he had just one arm. He did not go after a quick pin like the other boys, but rather began to knock Leo around the mat. Leo did his best to fend off the other boy but was getting beaten. As the opponent saw Leo tiring, he went in for the kill, and quickly Leo wrapped him up like he did the other boys and pinned him. He did the one move he had mastered, and it worked each and every time. Leo pinned his opponent and was a champion. He raised his left arm in victory.

Hugs and congratulations followed from Coach Jones and his parents. After they placed the medal on Leo's chest, he began to feel some self-doubt. He asked Coach Jones, in front of his parents, "Did those boys let me win because I had one arm? Was this a set up to make me feel better?" Coach Jones quickly responded, "Leo, you absolutely won each and every one of those matches. You trained with me for six months with one move. You came every day dedicated to being the best you can be with the gift that God has given you and you won those matches fair and square. What you didn't know going into the tournament is that the only way to get out of the one move I showed you is by grabbing the opponent's right arm and pulling it backward. With no arm to grab, your opponents were at a loss and could not get out of the one move that you mastered. What you thought was your greatest weakness, we made your greatest strength. Congratulations and never doubt yourself. You earned each one of these victories today and should be proud of yourself."

Make an effort to turn what seems to be your child's perceived weakness into a strength. Self-confidence and fear of failure go hand-in-hand, especially when children think they are weak in an area. Build their confidence by focusing on positive perspectives. We have seen stories of success over and over and over with people facing their fears.

An inspirational movie, *The King's Speech*, illustrates this point very well as the King overcomes his speech impediment. We must not feed into our children's anxieties over what they perceive as a weakness. Share the story with them and have them turn what they think is their greatest weakness into a strength. With a positive mindset, a growth mindset, and the belief that no matter how bad the situation is, your children cannot fail, and only good things can come from that situation even in a loss.

22. DR. GILBERT'S TOP TEN TIPS FOR STUDENTS TO BE SUCCESSFUL

Dr. Rob Gilbert is a lifelong educator and a sports psychologist from Montclair State University. He is a good friend, mentor, and the creator of the success hotline. He has been leaving a 3-minute message about success each day on the hotline since January of 1992.

So many of his influences are weaved into these concepts to help you and your children. Give the hotline a try. 973-743-4690

- **Show up**
- **Pay attention**
- **Ask questions**
- **Ask for help**
- **Help others**
- **Take great notes**
- **Review your notes**
- **Do the work**
- **Do not cheat**
- **Do not quit: Do not allow your children to quit jobs, activities, or things they have signed up for.**

This last one is a life rule and a very important one. One they will remember forever. There is a difference between choosing to not do an activity after it is completed versus quitting in the middle of it. You must teach your children to see things through: live up to the commitments they have made, so later in life, when things get tough, they will have learned how to handle obstacles and difficulties. College life, marriages, jobs, and so many other life experiences will present with temptations to quit; it happens all too often, and we as parents need to teach our children how to see things through to completion.

I share this story with many, and there are so many lessons for me in it. It is about the day that my Dad died. My father had diabetes most of his adult life. He lost his eyesight, had colon cancer, and dealt with high blood pressure as well as many other elements associated with diabetes. Eventually, he needed a kidney transplant, and my brother courageously stepped up and donated a kidney to my father, as I wrote about earlier in the book. This changed his life and reinvigorated him. He lost weight and one day decided to walk a marathon. We all thought he was crazy.

Well, he did it with the help of the group Achilles International. This is a group founded by Dick Traum in 1983 that assists and supports disabled athletes. Learn more at achillesinternational.org.

My dad really became very interested in his health and exercise as he prepped for the marathon. He walked days and nights in the heat and cold. Always walking. Always wanting to walk a little bit faster. We wound up doing four marathons together, but in 2008 it was different. My Dad was not his usual self during that race and continued to say, "Let's not worry about the time today but let's just worry about finishing." He took many breaks that day and drank more water than usual. We carried him at times with him leaning on our shoulders, yet he continued to walk.

He kept saying, "We have to finish. Let's make sure we finish. Keep on walking." We offered several times for him to bow out of the race, but he would have none of it. When he completed the race that November of 2000 in seven hours and 50 minutes, little did we know that would be his last one.

We hugged goodbye, and I was off to northeast Pennsylvania, and he went back to Staten Island. He died that evening at home as he always said he wanted it to happen. He was definitely having a heart attack during the race yet never said anything because he wanted to make sure he finished it. *Do not quit, no matter the circumstances.* I miss my dad every day since his passing, but I will never forget this advice during all that I do. As in the Frank Sinatra song, my dad did it his way!

A second story that I recall about quitting is from my friend, a lifelong educator, and coach. Let's say his name was Mike. Mike was a lifelong athlete as well. He has been around sports and involved in sports his whole life. Mike played football and baseball in college, always on the field, always practicing. In his sophomore year of college, Mike injured his shoulder during the football season. It never really healed well, and he had continual pain into the baseball season, which hampered his performance on the team. This landed him on the bench, which frustrated him even more. Mike was a great athlete and was used to playing and succeeding in the field. In his frustration with not being able to play, he told the coach he was quitting. He turned in his uniform and left.

That night he realized what he had done and was very upset with himself. He loved the sport and had to be part of it. The next day he went back to the coach and told him he changed his mind and that he was coming back to the team. The coach looked him in the eye and said, "Absolutely not. You quit, and that's that. You can't just come back like that."

Mike was shocked and devastated. It hit him like a punch in the face. He became very angry and frustrated with the coach because he would not allow him back. It was not until years later that he realized this was one of the greatest lessons he had learned from his old baseball coach about commitment, actions, and the consequences of quitting activities. Mike shared the story with many of his athletes as a teaching tool over the years. Teach your kids not to quit.

23. SUPPORT THE SCHOOL FINANCIALLY.

A cup of coffee or brownie at the bake sale. A candle from the senior class fundraiser. The 50-50 at the ball game. Whatever it is, take a few dollars out of your pocket and continue to support the school financially. These monies are important for different opportunities for students, and the generosity of many is a great help to them. My Dad used to say to me that he wanted a trip to the Great Wall of China to make up for all of the two, three, four, and five-dollar donations and entrance fees that he paid over the years. I laugh and think of my dad and mom a lot as I work the bake sale at the school plays and buy the tickets for 50-50s. If money constraints are tight, and I understand certainly they can be, we can do the best we can to help support the school financially.

I look at it as one of those life rules of kids when they sell lemonade. You might really dislike lemonade, and it's the warmest, most watered-down lemonade you've ever seen or tasted, yet it is almost a must to give that kid that $.50 or a buck for the lemonade.

24. THE SCHOOL ASSIGNMENT THAT DOESN'T MAKE SENSE

Many times students will ask, "Why am I doing this assignment? When will I ever use this again?" Maybe use this true story to remind them of the reason when they ask these questions.

During a college class, the assignment was to find a foreign newspaper in New York City and cut out an article of interest. It did not have to be in another language. While Sid (the student)l did not see a lot of purpose for the assignment, he did it and found a short article about a rock band in Great Britain. The next week it was the same assignment. Sid did the same thing and found another article about the same rock band. He was very curious about them and intrigued by what the article shared about their amazing rock concerts. The third week, the third assignment, and this time it was a full-page article. Sid always loved rock 'n' roll and really became interested in the band. This was in the 1960s, and there was no internet yet. In one of the articles, Sid found the manager's name. He was able to contact the manager and discuss bringing the band to perform in NYC. Several months later, many, many phone calls, and after a lot of work, Sid helped arrange The Beatles' first stadium concert in the United States on August 15, 1965!

Sid Bernstein went on to become a very successful music manager and mogul in the business. Was it that assignment that sparked his interest? Was it that assignment that was the push that Sid needed to get started on a passion he did not even know he had?

The story is from the great Dr. Rob Gilbert and Success Hotline. Dr. Gilbert goes on to explain the law of unintended consequences. While the teacher may have had a different objective for that assignment, it found great meaning for Sid and uncovered a passion he may have never discovered. He also may have never found the Beatles, so don't whine and complain about an assignment just yet. Maybe it will pique your child's interest and create something for them that they did not have or know before the assignment!

25. CHUNK THE WORK.

From my days of refereeing, my mentors and top advisers told me, "Andrew, you don't have to ref the whole game. You just have to ref four minutes at a time." A college basketball game is broken up into 40 minutes. There are four scheduled timeouts in the first half and five in the second half, each of which is four minutes apart. (The first called timeout in the second half becomes a full media timeout.) So I trained myself, my mind, and my focus to be just four minutes each. Be my best until that next time out. Don't look at the clock and say I have to ref for 40 minutes. That perspective could be overwhelming. I tell this story because the same can go for school. Sometimes the year can be daunting. Oh my God, it's only September, and I have to go to school until June? It must be broken up into more manageable segments of time. For example, September until the first holiday either at the end of the month or Columbus Day, then to Veterans' Day or Election Day, to Thanksgiving, Thanksgiving to Christmas, Christmas to winter break or Martin Luther King or Presidents' weekend, to Spring Break, Spring break until Memorial Day, and lastly, Memorial Day until the end of the school year. These are natural breaks that occur during the school year that can help keep your child focus, not for the entire 40 weeks, but approximately just three-week segments of time. You can even offer incentives to further enhance motivation, such as if you get A's on every assignment between now and that break, we'll go see that movie you've been excited to see. Or, if you read 30 minutes a night for this timeframe, I'll get you those boots you wanted. #SmallVictories

Another aspect of the chunking mindset is the work. The best teachers do it for you when assigning longer projects. They require certain parts of the project done at certain times and have checkpoints. There will most likely be appropriate penalties for lateness through-out, but they will be clearly defined. Then again, some teachers have the college mindset of, *here's the assignment, here's what you must accomplish, and it is up to the student to determine how best to "chunk" it up*. Well, as we all know, most people procrastinate until the last minute—that Sunday night, when you're scrambling around running to Walmart to get supplies and up until midnight to complete this project that was assigned six weeks ago. Help your child chunk the work. Break it up by time and categories. What is the topic that you are discussing? What has to be completed and by when? How do you plan to organize the project? Have you made a list of materials and supplies? What will make the project unique or stand out? Try to guide your children to adapt to the long-term task to suit their personal schedule and work habits. My kids have had a variety of projects. As they've progressed through their education, I have found this extremely helpful. Not only for my wife and me but for the kids themselves. #ChunkTheWork.

26. DO A LITTLE A LOT OF THE TIME, NOT A LOT A LITTLE OF THE TIME.

Many of us have heard the saying, "How do you eat an elephant? One bite at a time." This is so true and really can be a valuable tool for children and young adults. Things can seem overwhelming. Things can seem too big and too hard to tackle, but it seems more and more people give up too easily. They give up on marriages, trying to accomplish amazing goals, etc. Teach your child this skill: *to do a little bit a lot of the time.* Not do a lot of the time. This concept will build skills of consistency, scheduling, and focusing on accomplishing a goal. My friend, Dr. Robert Zayas, the Director of the New York State High School Athletic Association, told me an amazing story of how he got his doctorate. He was struggling with his time and trying to get it all done. He had a young family and was trying to write his dissertation. About to throw in the towel, he decided to do it 30 minutes a day. Just 30 minutes a day. This lasted over several years, but slowly, slowly, and slowly he chipped away at it till eventually he completed it and now has his Doctorate. Such an encouraging story to share about what can be accomplished with the productive use of just 30 minutes a day!

Another success story is the origin of the Success Hotline (973-743-4690, thesucesshotline.com). I mentioned Dr. Robert Gilbert throughout this book, who, in just three minutes a day, has helped transform my life and the lives of so many others. He started on January 22, 1992, leaving a three-minute message about success. This was an assignment for his students to call into the hotline and then leave their thoughts. (He leaves a three-minute message; callers have one minute to leave Dr. Rob comments.) He got such great feedback and so enjoyed it himself that he has continued each and every day. He is on recording number 10,800+ (at the time of publication) and still going! I have been calling for over five years and just those three minutes a day, writing down these tips and stories has led to such a positive impact on life. It has brought such changes and growth. Think about all the one-day workshops and seminars you have participated in, the speeches that were awesome, moving, inspirational, and powerful; yet, did they really change your life? Actually, the little things that we do each day are what changes our lives. Teach your child to do a little a lot of the time, not a lot, a little of the time.

27. FORMING A HABIT

What habits do you want to instill in your child? I hope that after reading this book, you will take a few of the suggestions that work for you and your family and get rolling with forming habits with your child. So how do you do it? A little bit each day. If you want your child to eat more greens and vegetables, you know it just doesn't start with a plate full of vegetables and saying go ahead. Help form those habits through daily practice. Try different varieties of salads and different types of lettuce. My oldest does not like arugula, yet my son Matthew can't get enough of it. We've tried different dressings, adding nuts, seeds, and raisins as well as preparing them in different ways. My wife cooks an amazing sauteed spinach with garlic and olive oil. She recently started using the Ninja blender and blends green smoothies for the kids with pineapple. They can't get enough of it! We also make an effort at each meal to have green on the plate.

What about the habit of reading each day? A few years ago, after walking off the stage at graduation with the Valedictorian's family, I asked the father, "How did you do it? How did you get your child to be such an exceptional reader?" He looked at me very simply, smiled, and patted me on the back, saying, "Just a little bit each day. We made her read at least 30 minutes a day since she was young. She developed a love of reading, and off she went. We did not have to do much after that." I know it can be a battle with video games and Netflix these days, yet fight that battle. It is worth it. Get your children going with books on topics they are interested in—not necessarily for school but for the love of learning and the love of reading. Visit your local library and even have them walk around with the librarian to discuss topics they like, movies they're interested in, or anything they enjoy. The librarian will certainly help you and suggest numerous books for your children. Make it a daily ritual or habit to have them read. As it says in the title of this tip, a habit starts with a small thread. It starts with a few minutes a day that can turn into a lifetime of reading. Whatever the habit is that you would like to develop in your children, regardless of age, get them going with it just a little bit each day. Be consistent, and at first, you probably will have to make them do it. Start small and take baby steps and, if they do it each day, it certainly will become a habit, and then, hopefully, it will stay with them throughout their adult lives and even be instilled in the next generation.

CONSISTENCY, ACCOUNTABILITY, & ORGANIZATION

W e want accountability and responsibility for our children, but how will they learn if we don't hold them accountable for their actions. Accountability is like a strong rope: it is not made whole as one piece, yet many small fibers put together as one. These fibers are the experiences of our lives, many found in this chapter.

28. SIX NAILS

Meet Ms. Garcia (I have changed the names of many in the book for privacy reasons. All agreed for me to share their story, yet some wanted to not use their names). Ms. Garcia is a single mom, with three beautiful daughters, from the Dominican Republic. They moved to Port Jervis, NY, when her oldest was a junior, and the other girls were in middle school and elementary. In one meeting I had with mom, we talked about the girls' academics and their progress in school. She said to me in a very passionate and determined voice: "Mr. Marotta, I have six nails on my wall: one for each of their high school diplomas and one for each of their college diplomas. That's the expectation. That is the standard—my standard. They know it, and we talk about it often. Their education is everything, and we as a family will work towards these goals together." I was extremely impressed by this—not just the goal itself, but the passion that Ms. Garcia had for her daughters and this goal of a college diploma for each. I think the nails are a powerful reminder to this family and a story I thought important to share in this book.

What are your nails for your child, and how will you communicate them?

29. TAKE BACK WHAT IS THEIRS: CARTER'S STORY.

Carter was a very easy-going kid, yet tough. He had a quiet confidence about him, was responsible, and very hardworking. Carter's headphones were stolen out of the locker room. He was upset, reported it to us, and went about his business. The next night, he was at the basketball game at the HS, and he saw a boy who was wearing his headphones. Carter was smart enough to have taken a picture of the serial number of the headphones and had that number on the ready. He approached the boy calmly and said, "Those are my headphones." The boy, of course, denied that the headphones were indeed Carter's. Carter whipped out the serial number, showed it to the boy, and again, calmly demanded the headphones back. He was not confrontational, disrespectful, nor too forceful, yet serious and focused. The boy, knowing he had been outsmarted, reluctantly handed back the headphones.

I was very impressed with Carter's handling of this situation: his disposition, his courage, and his calm throughout the whole thing. He never got crazed or over angry about the incident yet just got his headphones back. Most times, these types of conflicts will end in some sort of fight or have a negative outcome. His demeanor, confidence, and having wisely taken a picture of the serial number all led to his getting the headphones back—no drama, no fight, and no showing off in front of others. He simply did what he had to do and got the headphones back. To me, this was a great example of a young man handling his business and righting a wrong without making a big fuss. I congratulated him and his parents on the incident and followed through by disciplining the young man who had, indeed, taken the headphones.

30. IF THEY BREAK IT, THEY BUY IT. IF THEY LOSE IT, THEY REPLACE IT.

Accountability. Responsibility. Understanding the value of money. All of these are traits we want our children to have, and how can we assure that they do? By enforcing this mindset. Certainly, accidents will happen, and things may be out of their control, especially if we allow carelessness. They must be taught discipline in how they treat their own belongings and the possessions of other kids. They must not be careless with things.

As they grow older, they will learn that if they are held responsible for their items, they will take better care of them. If they lose their sneakers because they left them in the locker room and you just run out and buy another pair, why would they treat that new pair any differently than the ones that they lost? If they are made to wear older sneakers or maybe ones that were put aside for yard work or things like that when it's time for a new pair, they will be more responsible. If they get mad because they lost at a video game and throw the remote control and break it, is it the parents' responsibility to replace it? I think not. Jonny will learn very quickly to take better care of it when he does not have a remote to play his game.

Out of all my children, my son Matthew is the most money-conscious since the first time we made him pay for something he lost. It was his sneakers, and he left them at practice. He was upset, and I told him he would be responsible and, if he wanted new ones, he would have to pay with his own money. He went upstairs, got the cash, came downstairs, and very slowly put it on the table. He apologized for losing the sneakers and said he would be more mindful in the future. We told him good and that we would order him new ones because he was paying for them. I know it was very difficult for him to put that money on the table, and it was challenging for my wife and me to make this happen but, in the end, we knew it was best to help teach him the value of his possessions and the money that these items cost. He has been more mindful and also does not want that to happen again.

While it may be a challenge for you and your family to start this if you don't do it already, you will be happy you did in the long run because it does teach your child accountability and responsibility.

31. NAME YOUR PRICE FOR SNOW SHOVELING.

When I was around nine or ten years old, I got my first paper route. I loved it and became heavily involved in the route, my customers, and just the day to day things that would come up while doing the route. Customers started to ask me if I could water their flowers while they were on vacation, walk the dogs, and even start to paint and do odd jobs around the house. Out of this, my first company, Handy Andy, was born! This, too, I loved. Developing relationships with people in the community and making money were both very invigorating and energizing for me.

When winter hit, I started to pick up snow shoveling jobs as well. One of my first experiences was at an elderly woman's home who lived by herself. She was a very nice woman whom I was happy to help. On this particular morning, we probably had a foot of snow, maybe fourteen inches. School was canceled, and I was out early to make some money. I knocked on her door, asked her if she would like me to shovel, and she said, "Of course!" and I went at it. It was probably an hour and a half of heavy shoveling. I busted my butt and was exhausted. I knew I had some more homes to take care of and more money to make.

When I knocked on the door to tell her I was done, she smiled at me and handed me four dollars. I thought she was kidding and was going to whip out another 20, but she told me to enjoy the snow, and she shut the door. I stood there in shock and then began to get angry. How could she have only paid me four dollars when I just busted my butt doing that hard labor for at least an hour and a half? That job was easily worth $20-$30. She had a double-wide, long sidewalk and a winding path to her door. I cleared every inch of it. My emotions went from angry to frustrated to upset, and all the while, I huffed and puffed.

When I returned home after shoveling, I expressed my anger and frustrations to my parents. They listened patiently. When I was done venting, my Dad looked at me and said, "What price did you give her before you accepted the job?" I looked at him and said I didn't give a price, that is what she gave me. He then again asked, "Why would you have accepted a job without negotiating the price ahead of time?" I told him I wasn't sure but just assumed she would pay me a fair rate.

He said that it's your fault that you did not negotiate the price ahead of time.

He continued by stating I should have looked at the job, estimated how long it would take me, and then set the price either right down the middle or preferably a little bit towards my side money-wise. The only person I was to be angry at was myself.

I learned a valuable lesson that day and from then on always gave a price ahead of time for any of my jobs, which I continued into my college years. I made a lot of money, a lot of friends, and learned about building trust and relationships with people. So the reason I share this story is that it is important for your child to work: Small jobs, part-time jobs, different jobs, whether it is babysitting, catering at different events, or working at the local pet shop, your child should be empowered to set their price. Obviously, if they are working at a chain restaurant or a place that has a set pay, that's different. If it is a small place or a single owner where they are being paid under the table (cash only), they should not be afraid to negotiate their pay.

32. LET THEM WORK IT OUT.

I have many situations that happen at school where parents call me directly. They want to go right to the top and handle a situation for their child. Many times I direct my secretary to ask the question, "Have you spoken to the teacher? Have you spoken to the coach? Has your child spoken to the teacher or coach? I believe that is what we want. We want the child to try to work it out with the adult for themselves. This may vary at different ages and in certain situations. You may have to jump in sooner rather than later but, in many cases, empower your child to work it out, whatever it may be.

Let's say the situation is your child is not happy with the grade they received on an exam and maybe the grading wasn't all that clear.

How does this play out? Do you have a conversation at home with your child regarding the test and their preparation? Did they study? Were they prepared? How was the assessment? Those are all questions for a conversation for you and your child. Next, you encourage them to ask questions during class if there is a review. There are many students out there that are afraid to ask questions, yet many of the students probably have the same questions. Empower your child to show confidence by raising their hand and saying, "Hey Mr. Teacher, can you go over number 36? I didn't really get it. Thank you." That is a powerful thing for any child at any grade level to do.

Next, have your child speak with the teacher immediately after class and ask if they can go over the exam further after school. This is going to do many things. One, it will show the teacher that the student cares and is into doing well in school. Two, it will increase conversation and understanding between the teacher and the student. Three, it will help build the relationship between the teacher and the student. And hopefully, it will help your child gain a greater understanding of the content, where they went wrong, and maybe is there a possibility for test corrections, extra credit, or something to maybe earn some of the points back on the exam depending on the grading policies and flexibility of the teacher. Most times, only good things can come from this type of conversation.

After that, you should follow up with your child to see what the outcome was and did they make any progress in terms of understanding the content better, and any additional information regarding the test. This was 100% student-driven and, even though you may have been behind the scenes, this is empowering for your child and can take them a long way in preparing the future concerning how to handle struggles when they occur in college. How about when there's a conflict with an employer? Are you going to go in there before your child has ever advocated for themselves? Let them work it out, and if you have to step in later after they've done all of those steps, then so be it, but strengthen your child's confidence and communication skills by challenging them to go to the teacher directly. This is a very important component of your child's education and overall social well-being.

33. PROBLEMS THEY HAVE IN SCHOOL MAY BE THE SAME OR SIMILAR PROBLEMS THEY HAVE LATER IN LIFE.

I have seen this too many times over my career. The good news is when positive things are happening and bright flags of hope and indicators of success, most likely, that student is going to go on to do great things in their future. Unfortunately, the opposite is also true. In a general sense, if a student uses drugs or abusing alcohol in their middle school and teenage years, we tend to see these issues later in life. I dread picking up the paper and seeing a drug overdose death or drunk driving accident of a former student with whom we had those same issues. I battled many parents who argued with me and fought with me as I tried to help their child and help them understand that we were not out to get their kid but rather seeing warning signs of poor behavior. Some parents were able to accept the insights and get help, while others wanted to blame us for trying to harm their child because, for some reason, they thought we didn't like them.

Additionally, this goes for other negative behaviors such as reckless driving, domestic abuse, stealing, and others. If your child displays these behaviors early in their pre-teen and teen years, you have to be firm and fair and not tolerate them. The longer behaviors are allowed to continue, the greater chances they have to manifest themselves in your child's behaviors as they grow. Fight the battles now. Take the phone now. Ground them now. Even though it is hard, these are battles that are easier when they are younger. As I have written multiple times in this book, when you look back, will you say, "I'm glad I did," or "I wish I had?"

34. ADD: ATTENTION DEFICIT DISORDER

by Jennifer Marotta, my wife. Jenn is also an amazing elementary guidance counselor in Delaware Valley Schools in Milford, PA, our hometown.

Our son, Matthew, is a bright, funny, and hard-working sweet boy. He is energetic, enthusiastic, and fast. Fast at everything he does…sounds great? Well---let me rephrase that. He has strong ADD tendencies. I did not always have this solidified in my mind. I remember a time where I was yelling all too often at him. This was around the age of three- to five-years-old. I was frustrated that he didn't remember things, directions, his shoes, or if he washed his hands or not. He was so different from his older sister. He was so different from me. I wasn't sure what to do, but I knew I didn't want to have this dynamic with him. We have a long road together so I needed to pave it differently.

I look for patterns when I'm stuck, patterns in behaviors and within relationships (guess that's my counselor hat that's creeping in). I looked at the environment, conditions, and time of day when these exchanges of frustration would occur. I started to see patterns. He was doing a benign activity when I was talking to him; he was daydreaming, he was watching a muted screen, he was thinking of another question to ask me. It was like he was changing the channel in his head during a conversation, like he was joining us "via satellite," like that older news feed when the reporter on the scene would respond a bit delayed. Through the years, he and I had looked for these patterns during calmer times when we were not rushed, hungry (that's a big one!), or tired. We are very different people, and I love how we interact now because of the small changes. I touch his shoulder and ask him if he is "ready." He now knows that I need his attention. He does well with these small redirects. They work for him, and now he is in a much better place, and I am happily a little less frustrated. —*Jennifer Marotta*

(Andrew writing) I'm grateful to my wife for working with Matthew through these struggles. It is important, whatever the issues that our kids are facing, that we help them find workarounds, ways to get around the hurdles. The hurdles and challenges will always be there, yet it is the response to these situations that define people and allows those who can develop workarounds to move forward.

35. YOUR KID MIGHT HAVE A DIFFERENT EXPERIENCE THAN YOU DID.

You may have loved art. You might've had a problem reading. You may have had an embarrassing situation in PE class or have been the leading scorer on the basketball team. You may have starred in the play or been as shy as a newborn cub. Whatever your experience was in school, your child might be different. Be mindful of expecting the same for your child as when you went through school. A lot has changed since then, and they may be different than you, in a different school, and certainly at a different time. Just because you may have struggled in algebra, does it mean your child has to? They may have a different teacher, they may start working at it earlier, or they might love math. Be mindful of these differences, especially your negative experiences. Do not create anxiety or fear for your child because you may have had a bad situation in school. Things are also very different these days. A lot of collaborative learning, a lot of technology, and a lot more student voice and choice are happening in schools today. You may be a parent from the generation when the teacher lectured for an hour at a time. Those days are over, and school is very different now. See what your child's experience is all about, listen to the things that they like as well as their struggles, and be mindful that their experience will most likely be different than yours.

36. THEY ARE NOT TOO OLD FOR A BEDTIME.

Rest, rest, rest. Your child is growing and developing. Even if they are a teen and look grown to you, they still are developing. This is so important. Building bedtimes and starting early will set your child on pace for a good night's sleep. Setting the bedtime and not allowing the electronics in the bedroom in the evening time are essential to creating good sleep habits from which there can only be positive outcomes. There are many discussions and debates about different parenting styles and suggestions about nighttime routines. Still, I don't think there is an argument against setting a bedtime, even for high school-age children. Start early and stick to it, especially during the week. Weekends you have some flexibility and fun times for the kids to stay up a bit later, but come late Sunday afternoon, start to wind it back down and get ready for that very important bedtime

37. HOOT WITH THE OWLS.

Ron Semerano was a lifelong educator and coach in the Port Jervis School District. We had many conversations about everything over the years, and I have learned a great deal from him. He shared this story about a night when he and his dad stayed out too late. He described having been out way too late the night before, and a call came in the morning to substitute teach. His dad answered the call, and Ron said he wasn't going to go in because he was too tired. His dad told the sub caller that Ron would be in shortly, hung up, and promptly grabbed Ron out of bed. He told him to get dressed and go to work. He then shared this amazing quote about responsibility, respect, and time management: "I want you to fly with the eagles. If you want to hoot with the owls at night, you better get up and fly with the eagles in the morning." This had a profound impact on Ron's life and he has remained an early riser throughout his adult life. Of course, he was never late for anything and not only flew with the eagles, but also became one in all he did!

38. FOCUS ON EFFORT AND NOT THE OUTCOME. FOCUS ON THE PROCESS AND NOT THE RESULT.

A "B" on that science project, an A-minus on the writing assignment, a "C" on the math test. Your kid will have hundreds, if not thousands, of assessments, tests, projects, and more over the years, whether they are in first grade or twelfth grade. There will always be assessments that have a grade attached to them. Grades can cause kids and families anxiety and stress. My advice to you is to put your focus on effort and doing the best you can during the process. How often and when do your kids study? Is there a phone in the same room with them? Does music help them or hurt them? Are they studying to get a grade on the test, or are they studying to learn and have a greater understanding? These are all important questions, and yes, I certainly understand that those grades are necessary and are the end-all-be-all for a lot of things like honors classes, college admissions, and National Honor Society requirements. If your child is prepared, feels confident, and has put the time in, the end result should be a positive one. Think about that last project they had. When did they receive the assignment? Did you sit down with them and help them build a graphic organizer that includes dates, materials, etc.? Did you have them put in an hour a day over a two-week period, or did they cram all day Sunday going into Sunday night that caused stress and frustration for all parties involved? It's the process, it's the time, but it's the organization of the work that will help with the positive outcome of a good grade. If you do this test after test and project after project, I know your child will be successful. If, indeed, a poor grade results, what then are the questions you ask? Do you push right away, or do you sit down together and rewind the tape? Go through their notebooks with them and look at the materials they had to study? Maybe ask the teachers for a copy of the assessment, or, if you could, review it with them and your child to see maybe where the gaps were and how you can do better next time. As I shared at the beginning of the book, this is a marathon, not a sprint, and it's important that you keep running, keep building confidence with your child and focus on the process, not necessarily the end result.

We've had our fair share of late Sunday nights where there were growls, dirty looks, and frustrations. After those events occurred, we regrouped. My wife and I, and the children involved, put things in place to correct the procrastination. Those negative scenarios can be your norm, or you can have a happy, confident child who chunked the work and built a calendar with their parents for their school project that included who is putting the project in the car Wednesday evening, and it's not due until Friday. That is a happy child, a happy wife, and a dad that feels good about all of that.

How do you know where you are going if you do not set the course? I have found that children will most times reach the bar that is set for them, not necessarily every time, but most times for most kids. Here are a few examples: quarterly goals on their report card, saving up money for Christmas or vacation, making the National Honor Society or an athletic team, or getting into college. Set goals with your children. An important aspect is that you are doing it with them, not for them. Talk to your children about what they feel they can accomplish. Do not be afraid to push them and make some goals that might be hard to reach. Have the mindset of a quote from my friend Dr. Rob Gilbert, "If you shoot for the moon and miss, you will land among the stars."

My oldest, Claire, is in middle school, and she was so proud when she got the Presidential Award at school for academic excellence. She had set this goal on her own and kept it to herself. When she got the certificate, she was beaming with pride because it is something that she wanted to accomplish and set out to do it. We were so proud of her and took her for a special treat for her achievement. It is important to celebrate the successes and keep your child motivated.

After you set them, the goals should be posted where your child can see them often. They should be written clearly and simply. You may not be necessarily creating "Smart goals" (specific, measurable, attainable, relevant, and time-bound), but you should be checking in with your child regularly on their progress. Celebrate the goals they achieve and listen to them if they don't make the goals to try to find out why. Remember, as I wrote in the first tip in this book, you are running a marathon, not a sprint, so there will be many more ups and downs, conversations to be had, and goals to be set and achieved.

39. ORGANIZATION, ORGANIZATION, ORGANIZATION

This is one of the great challenges of parenting, regardless of how old your child is. You might be lucky and have one that is organized but usually, this is a challenge for kids. Where did they put that assignment? Where did they write down that assignment? Where did they put the project list? Sports equipment for after school? Only have one cleat, missing the shin guard, only have one sock? Seen it all. Spirit week, and you're supposed to wear green? The five dollars for the teacher gift due on Wednesday, and the PTA president is emailing you? Organize, organize, organize their stuff, the calendar, the menu, and of course, the work. Slow the train down and get organized.

Whether that is the big wall calendar hanging in the kitchen, kids sitting around the table with their devices in Google Calendar, redoing the cubby area, etc. —how do you tackle these hurdles with your family to make it all work? You've all seen those minivans at the school event or soccer game. The parent scrambling to get to the event coming five minutes late. The back trunk flips open, and a cleat, book bag, sandwich snack fall out, and the kid runs out of the car with a mismatched outfit and a disheveled look. The reason I know this is because that's been my family. You implement some of these practices that will help prevent these types of occurrences from happening. Being organized is super helpful in your journey. Here are some further tips from my cousin Denise and her family.

40. PLANNING IT OUT

By Denise Dicks

Denise is an NYC elementary teacher, a mom, wife, and overall an amazing person of character and integrity. She is also my first cousin, who I love dearly.

As a parent, I feel that being organized is one way to help my children be successful. Organization is key for a smooth-running family. Being organized has helped my family stay calm and focused in the busy world in which we live.

As a mother of two very busy children, I keep myself organized with the ever-important family calendar. When my girls were young, it was a simple daily organizer thrown into my bag. I used it to keep track of appointments, play dates, and sports schedules, as well as adult obligations. Now that things have gotten even busier, I use an app on my phone to help my family stay organized. It keeps track of the entire family's schedule, and every member has access to view and add events. I do not commit myself or a family member to any event until I check the date first. This is an easy way to be sure that you do not overschedule yourself or your children.

Another way I keep my family organized is by reviewing our schedules in advance. Every evening before settling in for the night, I quickly pull up the app on my phone to check the next day's schedule. I make sure we have everything we need ready to go for the next day. School uniforms are washed and laid out, sports equipment is packed and ready to go (even if that means a last trip down to the washer and dryer), $2 for ice cream at lunchtime is in the lunch box, all school work is put away and packed in the school bags. This helps make the dreaded mornings a little less hectic and eliminates frantic phone calls during the day about missing homework, cleats, or other necessities.

I believe this type of organization has made a lasting impression on my children. They know what is expected of them, and it has helped to ease anxiety in their hectic lives. My hope is that they will take this trait of mine and continue to use it in their lives as they become adults and have their own families. Now, if I could just get my 15-year-old to keep her room organized—that would be a miracle! But that's a story for another day!

—*Denise Dicks*

41. HAVE YOUR CHILD FIND A PART-TIME JOB/SUMMER JOB (PREFERABLY DOING SOMETHING THEY LIKE).

The only time my folks gave us money was on vacation. They would always buy us something nice, and if we asked for something on vacation, the answer was usually YES! Other than that, we were on our own. We all had jobs as kids and into early adulthood. I can remember so many different jobs that have prepared me for my role as a father, husband, principal, and college basketball referee. As a kid, I worked at a gas station, a restaurant, shoveled snow, newspaper route, and even walked the ponies at the Staten Island Zoo! Each one of these gave me a different skill that I took with me later in life. Working at a basketball camp as a summer basketball coach inspired me to want to become a teacher and got me started in the world of education. It was the spark of teaching kids at that young age that got me going. Having jobs also teaches the kids a sense of responsibility, money management, people skills, and responding to supervisors, good and bad. There is so much value in our kids having jobs.

One of my good friends and mentors, John Xanthis, grew up working at his father's gas station in Newburgh, New York. It was one of those old-fashioned places where when the car rolled in and rolled over the line, the bell rang. John used to run out as a young boy, wash the windows, pump gas, clean the windshield wipers, and take care of the customer. He shared the story with me of how his father sent him home one day because he did not have enough zip in his step...and not hustling to customers and giving his best effort. He believed in the highest of service and respect for the customers.

John is one of the best educational leaders I know, and it is in strong part due to his relationship-building skills and his caring for people. Hmmm. I wonder where this came from?

42. IF YOU DO THE CRIME, YOU DO THE TIME.

Your kid is going to make mistakes. Your kid is going to get in trouble. Your kid is going to break some rules. It's natural, and it happens. As a parent, you certainly want to guide them in the right direction and correct wrongdoings.

When I was in the eighth grade, I attended the prestigious St. Joseph Hill Academy in Staten Island, New York. There were two grades per class or two classes per grade, and halfway through the year, there had been some building shenanigans going on in the cafeteria. An escalation of trouble culminated one Friday afternoon with a food fight. I remember grabbing cupcakes and whatever I could get my hands on and throwing it at all of the kids who also were participating. After some yelling by Sister Paulette, the All-Star authoritative cafeteria supervisor, she hauled eight boys to the Principal's office.

There were certainly girls that threw food, yet it was eight boys brought in for trouble. I remember the principal walking back-and-forth staring at us in her habit and eyeglasses, and a disappointed look. She told us we were all being suspended and that we had to call our parents. Each boy slowly and shamefully called one by one.

When it was finally my turn, I called my dad and told him what had happened, what I had done, and that he had to come to pick me up. There was a long pause on the other end of the line, and he did not say anything. I said, "Dad, you have to come to pick me up," and he said to me, and these words still ring in my ears today, "You got yourself in trouble, you get yourself out of it!" and hung up the phone.

The principal and I sat stunned at what had just happened. She looked at me and said, well what are you going to do? I looked back at her and said I don't know. She could not believe what my dad had done. I eventually called my Aunt Maryann, who scolded me on the phone yet would come and get me. She and my sister Suzanne would take care of me.

I learned a valuable lesson that day that I was responsible for my own actions and had to deal with the consequences of my behaviors. Mom and dad would not come and rescue me if I got in trouble. I remember I went out once before the time of cell phones (omg, I feel so old writing that!), and my dad would ask me, "Do you have a quarter?"

At first, I asked why? And his answer was always the same, "So you can call someone else if you get in trouble but don't call me!" Do not bail your kids out all the time if they get in trouble. If you are constantly running to their aid, how will they learn? If they know that mommy and daddy are always going to try to right their wrongs or rescue them when they get in trouble, how are they to learn?

In the end, I always knew my parents would support me and take care of me, but I also knew that if I got in trouble that I would have to deal with the consequences, and they would not come and rescue me. There is a fine line between love and support and overdoing it from which your children will not learn from their mistakes. Don't be afraid to punish or accept the punishment from others while dealing with mistakes your child makes. It's not easy at times, but I remember that story vividly from my eighth-grade year and, and while I knew my dad loved me, he was not going to bail me out for my poor behavior.

43. NOTHING GOOD HAPPENS AFTER MIDNIGHT.

I heard this my whole childhood, and now, as a school administrator and parent, I would agree. There's only going to be trouble after a certain time. Be firm with your child about pick up times and where they can be. There are times when it may be acceptable, such as an all-night graduation party or New Year's Eve, things like that, but, as a general rule, nothing good is going to happen after midnight. You say this to your teenagers enough times, they will get it in their head. When they are off at college or as young adults, they will need this too. Those crazy stories of watching the sunrise or going right to work after being out all night are fun to hear once in a while, but they shouldn't be the norm. Enforce a reasonable curfew early and often, and your child will learn how to respect the time and how to respect you.

44. DO YOU KNOW WHERE THEY ARE AFTER SCHOOL?

2:30 PM? 3:30 PM? It is like that public service announcement when we were kids: do you know where your kids are? Well, I am a proponent of your child having some free, unstructured time, but you should know where your child is and with whom they are hanging out. Are they walking through an area near the school that might not be the best part of town? Are they going to a friend's house where they are home alone, unsupervised, and maybe with boys and girls or young men and women?

In your weekly planning meeting with your child, these are things that should be asked and discussed. Who will be there, and what time will you be returning home or being picked up? Let them be kids and let them grow into responsibility but be aware of who, where, what, and how. Students that are not involved in a lot of school activities tend to look for something to do, and that can go bad in a hurry without positive influences and opportunities around them. Create those for your child by allowing them to join after school activities or outside clubs and making the commitment to pick them up, carpool with others, and/or arranging for transportation. These experiences can enrich the life of your child and maybe catapult them into something later in life. Also, those advisors, coaches, and kids can have a positive influence on your child just by being around them more often.

I attended basketball practices and camps for most of my childhood into my teens. This then led to an opportunity to play college basketball, which then rolled into an opportunity to officiate college basketball, a major component of my adult life. These experiences provided me tremendous opportunities to travel the world, bring my family along to experience traveling, and certainly provided some financial rewards. I think back to all of the pickups from these events as well as two, three, and five-dollar admissions that my parents paid for to attend the games.

In short, know where your child is after school and certainly encourage and help facilitate involvement in positive activities.

45. DON'T CURSE: SMASH THE CASSETTE STORY.

Rewind. I'm 12 years old. I am doing a chore that my parents had asked me to do, which was to paint the interior of our front porch. It was summertime, it was warm, and I had some music playing loudly on the old-fashioned boombox. The music had some explicit lyrics, and yes, there were a lot of curses. I did not think my dad was in earshot of the music, yet when he came up to me, I kind of said "Oh!" in my mind. My dad did not say anything. He came over to the boom-box, pressed stop on the cassette player (yes, we had cassettes way back then), dropped it on the ground, and then stomped his foot on it. He smashed the tape to pieces and then walked away. I sat there in shock with so many emotions running through my head: guilt, embarrassment, anger, stubbornness, and why the heck did he just do that? As a 12 or 13-year-old, I was mad at my dad for smashing my tape.

As I look back upon that experience now, I certainly understand why my dad did it and what he was trying to teach me. It might have been extreme, but that was consistent in many ways with who he was. The point of the story is to be mindful of what your kids are listening to, the content they are watching, and what they're feeding their brains. Once they get to a certain age, and with the invention of earbuds, this will be hard to manage but make an effort. Be involved. I've said this many times throughout the book that you do not want to be a helicopter parent managing everything that they are listening to or watching. Still, you should be mindful of harmful lyrics, explicit content, and too much too soon. They are kids, and they grow up fast, but do what you can to be mindful of what content your kid is absorbing.

46. YOU NEVER KNOW WHO IS ON THE OTHER END OF THE CALL.

At 10-years-old, my older sister was home with me, but my parents were out. This is in the mid-80s with no caller ID and certainly no cell phones. It was, however, the time of famous crank phone calls. The phone rang once, and the caller hung up on me. The phone rang again, with the caller hanging up on me. The phone rang a third time, and I let out an expletive that I certainly knew was inappropriate and wrong, yet I was trying to send a message for the person to stop calling. And it did the trick. The call stopped. About an hour later, my dad exploded through the front door, stomped down the hallway, and began pummeling me from all angles. In shock, not knowing what was going on, I screamed, "Stop! Stop! What are you doing?" He yelled, "Don't you ever, ever use that language again!"

I quickly realized that it was my dad on the other end of the line. This is back in the day of payphones. He was sticking a quarter in the machine, and obviously, it wasn't working. As with many of the experiences in this book, I certainly learned from my error and never spoke like that again on the other end of the line. Nowadays, with caller ID, cell phones, and such, people often don't even pick up the calls. I don't know who it's from. That being said, take the story, and you can relate it to so many areas. You're in the movie theater or out to dinner and speaking loudly. You never know who's sitting next to you. You're on a group chat on your phone and maybe don't know all of the numbers. Be mindful of what you're saying. You're at a party, and you don't know all of the guests, and you're talking loudly about someone or something. Maybe not the best idea. You never know

who's listening, and you never know where your words are going
to go.

47. IF YOU SUSPECT DRUGS OR ALCOHOL, BRING A STRONG, FAST-ACTING RESPONSE.

If you suspect drugs or alcohol, get after it. You are a parent, which
means you are a superstar. You know your child, and you know all
about them. If you suspect drugs, if you suspect sexual assault, if you
suspect drinking and driving, get after it. Passiveness in these situations will only delay or allow a bad situation to continue. You are not
your child's friend. You are not their guidance counselor. You are the
parent, and you need to confront the situations head-on. Do a little
research, do a little investigating, but certainly meet with your child
face-to-face and ask the question. Talk about honesty and the ability
to be open with one another. Trust one another and your expectation
to be told the truth in these different scenarios. You most likely will
be confronted with something like this along the way of this journey,
if you haven't already. Meet them head-on without fear or reserva-
tions, and be clear with your child. Do not beat around the bush.
These are very serious topics that could have detrimental effects on
your child. Show strength and be united with your husband, wife, or
partner in these scenarios.

48. IS IT DIFFICULT OR JUST TIME-CONSUMING?

This is another great concept from my friend Dr. Rob Gilbert. I love
this concept because it really makes so many things that seem compli-
cated, very simple. Put the time in. This is one of Dr. Gilbert's
favorite messages over the years. Nothing is difficult, just time-
consuming. Dealing with cancer or losing a loved one or pet is diffi-

cult. Having your house burned down is difficult. Divorce, addiction, etc. are all difficult, yet algebra, while challenging, is not difficult. Writing a term paper? Not difficult. This concept relates back to the chunking theory I wrote about earlier in the book. If you have this mindset of things being time-consuming, then have your child put the time in. Budgeting their time and yours can go a long way. Things like Facebook and binge-watching TV, etc., can eat up our time.

Did you know if you put an hour a day into something for five years, you will become one of the world's leading experts in that area? Furthermore, Dr. Gilbert has taught me over the years if it's something that you really do not like, implement the 15-minute rule. Your kid doesn't like doing the math homework? Make them do it for 15 minutes. You can give them a little break and then get back to it. Usually, when you start something and get engaged in it, you can keep rolling with it. It's the start that stops most people. I think this video illustrates this concept so perfectly. Take a look. I saw this from the great author and educator George Couros at one of his presentations. Although this is a Scotch commercial, it is the story that goes with this point. Give a watch. It's worth 3 minutes of your time.

https://youtu.be/Yy7fxLwfOnQ

This concept also reminds me of the story of the father whose daughter had kidney failure. He was 300+ pounds and way over the weight limit to donate a kidney. His daughter was given three to five months to live in her condition. The father needed to get to around 200 pounds to donate a kidney, which she very much needed. People said it was impossible. People said it couldn't be done. The father lost over 100 pounds in 2 1/2 months, and the family proceeded with a successful kidney transplant surgery shortly thereafter. Nothing is difficult, just time-consuming. Additionally, if you have a big enough "why," finding the "how" will be easy.

When your child watches Tom Brady win six Super Bowls and makes it look easy, they may think, "Wow! He's just really good," or "I can do that." Watching the Olympics and seeing swimmer Michael Phelps win all those gold medals, your child may say, "Wow! I can do that." And yes, they certainly can. Nothing is impossible, but you just have to put the time in. What about calculus? What about organic chemistry? All of those can be challenging subjects, and yet, if they studied each day for 30 minutes, they would get better at the subject and gain a better understanding. Port Jervis High School Hall of Fame teacher Kevin Birmingham always said review your notes for 15 minutes each night for each subject. Writing the notes first and then re-reading them will always have a great impact on your retention of the information.

Whatever the task, climbing Mount Everest, becoming a professional athlete, getting your doctorate, getting a 4.0 in college, becoming an engineer, whatever it is, if you teach your child to put the time in and dedicate themselves to their craft, they can do it. The great author Stephen King writes 2,500 words a day no matter what. Do you think that has to do with why he has written almost 100 books and is one of the world's most famous writers? Which came first, his writing every day or his becoming an excellent, famous writer? I believe the answer to be one and the same yet he continues on writing. So, when your children say that their seventh-grade math homework is difficult, have them put the time in to gain the understanding, and it will come.

49. FOCUS.

Jim was an older man who had gone to church his whole life. Several new families in the church had young children. More kids were crying, parents getting up, dropping items on the pews, and generally just making more racket. This really bothered Jim, and finally, he had enough after a long mass of screaming. He told the priest after Mass that he was leaving the church because of all the distractions, and the father asked him if he could stay a few moments while he said goodbye to the rest of the parishioners as they left the church. Minutes later, the priest met Jim in the quiet church, and he brought a full glass of water with him. He said, "Jim, I hear you regarding the distractions in church. I know sometimes the screaming can be frustrating. I brought you a glass of water."

Jim looked confused as he was not thirsty, just frustrated with the distracting children at Mass. The father said, "before you decide to leave the church, I'd like you to do one thing for me. Can you walk all the way around the back of the church, down the one aisle, and back up the other aisle while holding this glass of water and not spilling any?" Jim was very confused and asked the father why. He said, "I will explain afterward."

So Jim calmly took the cup and began walking very slowly. He watched the rim of the cup and kept his hand steady to not spill any of the water. The more he walked, the more focused he became on the cup and challenged himself not to spill any. He was halfway home and had not spilled a drop and started to walk back up the other aisle.

Jim was so pleased with himself as he rounded the corner and returned to the priest without one drop spilled. Jim handed the cup back to the father and said, "Okay. I'm done. What's your point?"

The priest said to him, "Why did you not spill any water?"

Jim answered, "Because I really concentrated on it and was focused on not dropping any because that's what you had asked me."

The priest said, "Well, I am now asking you to do the same with the mass and my homily regardless of what's going on during Mass. If you can focus on not spilling the water, you can focus on my words and God's message." Jim hugged the father and thanked him for the great story and activity of focusing on the water.

Your children will give you many reasons why they can't do something, and they have so many distractions in their lives. Especially in this age of tablets and cell phones, kids are more focused on those items than ever. Use this story as a teaching point when they become distracted. If you can get your child to focus on one thing at a time and commit to that focus, in time, this will help them, in the long run, to be able to navigate through all of the things they have for school and social activities. Block their time and have them focus on that one singular item until completion, just like Jim getting the water back to the priest in church!

TRUTHS

 The truth shall set you free"

— **JOHN 8.32**

I saw this quote above the doorway outside my high school, Xaverian HS, in Brooklyn, NY each day as I entered. It has always reminded me to tell the truth, even when uncomfortable. Help learn to empower your child to tell the truth in this chapter.

50. THE TALE OF TWO WOLVES

Reprinted with permission from Dan Spainhour's book, *Leading Narratives.*

A grandfather was discussing the ways of life with his grandson. He told him: There are two wolves that live within each of us one: one is a good wolf, joyous, kind, compassionate, and truthful. The other is not good. It is angry, selfish, and evades the truth. These two wolves are in each of us and fight all the time. The grandson had a troubled look on his face for a minute. He paused and asked, " Do I have these wolves inside me?" The grandfather replied, "of course," and then the grandson asked, "Which wolf will win?" The grandfather replied, "The one you feed."

I love this story. Can't you see the scene in your imagination: the grandfather and grandson sitting near a campfire, beautiful foliage in the background, birds and butterflies flying around with this profound conversation happening. This story has Native American origins and goes back in history. What does it mean? It means we all struggle with bad decision making at times. It means we've all succumbed to lying or poor choices at some point, and it is a struggle. You look at some people and think that they are just perfect. They're not perfect; they have just trained their wolves. They have been through the struggles and have chosen to make the better decisions or have learned from the poor ones they have made. Each experience is a new challenge, each day a new challenge: each new part of our lives presents more choices, hurdles, and in-fighting of our inner wolves. I challenge you to face the wolves inside you and talk to your children about this inner struggle early and often. The wolves will always be there, so train them early to help guide you through your journey and your children's journey.

51. FIRE, WATER, AND TRUST

When talking to your children about the concept of trust, regardless of their age, this is a great story to share. Fire, Water, and Trust were walking through the forest. They said to one another, "Hey, we should make a plan in case we get lost or separated." They all agreed it was a great idea. Fire said, " If you lose me, you can just look for the smoke and the glowing flames." Water said, "I'll be easy to find. Just look for the lush, green grass near the flowing creeks and brooks." Trust stated sadly, "If you lose me, I'm really hard to find again. You can work at it, but it may take a long time."

Trust is an important life trait we must constantly teach and demonstrate to our children daily. When we are confronted with situations with our children, we want to feel confident that their first reaction will be to tell us the truth, not lie because they are fearful of the consequences. Explain to them--what is worse? The act, the situation, or trying to cover it up?

52. ADMIT, FIX IT, AND MOVE ON.

Things are going to happen. Your kids are going to get caught up in circumstances, sometimes directly their fault and other times just because of their friends or situations in which they're involved. When that does happen, try to teach the concept of "admit it, fix it, and move on." You want to build trust and honesty not only with you but also with the school. It's better that your children be known for their honesty versus being a liar. Think about so many of the incidents that have happened in history, such as Watergate, deflate-gate, steroids in sports. The cover-up is always worse than the actual incident.

Situations are going to come up, and your kid is going to get in trouble. Continue to teach the concept of *Admit it, Fix it, and Move on.*

53. DON'T BELIEVE EVERYTHING YOU HEAR.

The teacher cursed at a student. Johnny peed in his pants in class. There was an emergency shelter in place drill. Sally got caught cheating on the exam. I'm being treated unfairly. These are all things that you may hear from your child when you asked the question, how was school today? Don't believe everything you hear. Not that your child would be lying to you or telling you something that wasn't true, yet this is like a game of telephone from back in the day. Your child may have heard something secondhand, and/or they were not really paying attention. From the thousands of student interviews I've done when there's been an incident in class, my experience is that most times, they do not recall the incident as it happened.

There have been fights in the hallway where I've conducted approximately 10 interviews because the film on the camera was not available at the time. I wrote down step-by-step details of what students said they saw. The next day our tech people were able to get the clip on the camera system, and I would say that on average, I get about 25% accuracy from student interviews of what really happened. Either they were on their phones, in conversation with someone else, or shocked by the whole incident and did not really get a grasp of what happened.

Do not jump to conclusions when your child tells you something or you hear something from another parent. Ask follow-up questions and dig deeper. Ask what exactly did Johnny say? Who did he say it to? Was the teacher there? What was the response? Tell me what happened afterward. Can you write down some of your thoughts for me to help better organize them? If you are still concerned after the follow-up questions, certainly a call or an email to an adult that was present may give you further clarification. The point is, don't over-react every time your child tells you something. It might not be 100% accurate or true.

I remember a game of Telephone that created a stir and some fear in a lot of people in the community in which I work. Sadly, Mr. Bird, a longtime technology teacher in our district, had passed away. As people spoke to one another and shared the news, someone said to someone else that Mr. Bird passed away. The person responded, "That's so sad that Mr. Burke passed away. I did not know he was sick." This conversation went on back and forth, and eventually, the second person of that conversation shared the news with others until another person called and posted and texted about sadly how Mr. Burke passed away. *Mr. Burke (not Mr. Bird)* is a parent and community member who works part-time in the district as a school monitor. I eventually got a call that *Mr. Burke passed away* and was greatly concerned as I have his daughter in school. I started packing my bags and getting my things together to go visit his daughter at the house as this was on the weekend. As I was getting ready to leave the house, I got another phone call describing the chain of events that occurred and the mistake made along the way: That it was Mr. Bird who passed away, not Mr. Burke!

Remember, everything you hear might not be accurate or true, so it is always best to confirm before you react.

54. FEAR: FALSE EVIDENCE APPEARING REAL

My friend and NY school leader Tom Bongiovi used to say this a lot when we worked together in Port Jervis. *False Evidence Appearing Real.* Don't get caught up in the gossip and don't believe everything you hear. Know the facts and learn about situations before you pass judgment or talk to your children about their teachers, the school, other students, or things going on in their lives. It is so easy these days to rush to judgment and make incorrect decisions about people. I hear this all the time as a school administrator and in my former role as a basketball official. I always laughed when I officiated, and I was in some obscure place, hours from home, or even in a different state. I would make a call that favors the home team, and someone will yell, "You're a Homer" from the stands? What? Homer? (someone who only roots for the "home" team.) How could you even say that when you have no idea where I'm even from?

It reminds me of the story of when I was officiating in Wichita, KS. The visiting team was from New Jersey, not far from Staten Island, NY, where I grew up. The team from Wichita was thumping the visitors, and the coach of the visiting team was getting quite frustrated that his team was losing so badly. He started to yell at my partners and me pretty good, yet was particularly coming at me harder and with more vengeance than the other two officials. He was saying things like, "I know how this works. You take care of the home team because you're never going to see me again!" "We're the road team, so we're going to get screwed."

I sprinted to him, went nose to nose, and said, "Coach! I have no idea what you are talking about, but I need you to know that I live within 30 minutes of your school and have never been to Wichita before in my life. Additionally, you and I are the only two Italians in this joint, so we have more in common than not! Don't make judgments that you don't know what you are talking about." He smiled, laughed, put his arm around me, and said, "thank you for speaking with me." He was a gentleman for the rest of the game.

Don't believe everything you hear, and don't let false evidence appear real. While working with your children along their educational journey, there will be things you like and things you don't like, but don't get caught up in rumors and things that aren't true. Know the facts and deal with the facts.

55. TELLING TALL TALES

A young boy in the town was spreading rumors and lies about some other children and adults. People brought this to the attention of the boy's parents, who then confronted their son. They brought their son to the wise Rabbi at the synagogue for some counseling. The wise Rabbi asked the boy about his lies and why he was telling falsehoods. The boy had no answer for the Rabbi. The Rabbi told him, here is your punishment: Go down to the river with a feather pillow. Rip one side of the pillow wide open and shake out all the feathers until they all are out of the pillowcase. Then come back and see me when you have done so.

Later that afternoon, the boy went back to the rabbi and told him he had completed the assignment. The rabbi had said you are only half done; now you must go back down to the river and collect the feathers. The boy looked astonished and asked, "How can I do that? They are all over the place." The Rabbi said, "So are your lies." From then on, the boy knew not to make up rumors or stories about others.

56. HOW DO YOU KNOW IF THEY ARE LYING?

How do you know when kids are lying? What are the clues? Why are some people better at determining it than others? One simple thing to look for is the repeating of your question with another question. They repeat the answer and say something like: Why would I take that phone? Why would I have eaten that last slice of pizza?

Here is a great article that I think points out some great things to look for. Hopefully, you won't need this a whole lot, but good to know for when you do.

http://bit.ly/BusinessInlying

I liked this article because it gave practical, easy to spot suggestions for you to look for. While it is not a perfect science, these tips can help you. In my experience, it is usually a combination of a number of these things, like the extra information, the shuffling of the feet, and the repeating of words, information, etc. Also, be aware that sometimes people just get nervous if they are being questioned about something, so keep that in your pocket also.

57. THEY WILL LIE: THE DENT IN THE PLYMOUTH FURY

I had to ask my sister's permission to tell the story and man; is it a funny one. It was December in the 1980s. This is back in the day when people regularly used snow tires. There was a storm approaching, and my dad told my oldest sister Suzanne to go bring the snow tires down to the street from the basement and put them in the trunk so he would get them switched with the regular tires the next day at the local mechanic. The next morning I heard my dad yelling about something and went down to see what was going on. There was a huge dent in the car with some beer bottles and such around the car.

My dad was frustrated at what happened. He asked Suzanne about the tires and if she had dented the car accidentally, and she said no, she did not. It looks like there had been some hooligans there that might've caused the damage, she said. He went off to work as he always did and then returned later that evening.

Later I found out that my mom and dad had questioned Suzanne once again, and she did indeed cause the dent. She was trying the best she could to lug these heavy snow tires down to the car but just couldn't manage it, so she decided to try to roll them down. The one got away from her and slammed into the side of the car, pounding down the steps. Suzanne was upset by what happened and afraid to tell my parents, so she got some debris from across the street and put it near the car. She also placed a beer bottle that she had found on top of the car. She was hoping that they would think it was vandals that caused damage to the car. I learned a lot from my parents over the years, and this story stuck with me for several reasons. They were not as mad at Suzanne about the accident as they were that she lied to them about what she had done. It really was an accident, and those tires were probably too heavy for Suzanne, yet my parents never took it easy on us and demanded that we do what they asked of us.

What I learned and remember from these incidents is that kids will lie. Suzanne was a great kid, has gone on to a very successful career in education, and is a fantastic writer. Yet even Suzanne, at that age, was capable of lies. I share this story because parents should be aware that children will lie. No matter how many times you tell them that you want the truth, if they believe they can get away with it, kids will lie. Not all kids, and please don't be offended that I am grouping kids together. Certainly, there is a large percentage of kids that generally tell the truth, but kids will lie. Be ready for it and don't be over-suspecting, yet keep that in your back pocket to know that no matter how good your kids are, they are capable of telling a lie. #SnowTires

58. WHAT'S WORSE: THE WRONG BEHAVIOR OR LYING ABOUT IT?

You could go back in history time and time again and look back at different scandals that have happened. Why are they scandals? In the mindset of 'admit it, fix it, and move on,' how do we develop an environment and culture in our families where our children will just be honest with us? Within the numerous incidents in history, what was worse: the actual incident itself or lying about it? Let's take the example of steroids in baseball. I grew up watching the Yankees. During my childhood, either the game was on the TV or on the radio 162 times a year plus, of course, all of the playoff runs! Let's take two great Yankee pitchers, Andy Pettit and Roger Clemens. If you are younger and these players were from before your time, certainly you can Google them to read the stories for yourself, but here's the story: Roger Clemens was probably the game's dominating and most intimidating pitcher for a period of six to ten years. He was a massive, physical specimen and had incredible speed and control. Later in his career, he certainly had increased muscle mass and amazing speed on his fastball. His name was mentioned so many times regarding steroids, and there was so much overwhelming evidence, including multiple different reports, investigations, and even a federal hearing. To this day, Roger Clemens still denies that he used steroids. There are interviews and accounts with unbelievable, specific details about his steroid use, yet Clemens consistently has denied it. You ask any sports fan who knows the story, and they will tell he used steroids, and most people think he's a liar.

The other side of the story is Andy Pettit. He was a tall, left-handed pitcher who won many games, including in the World Series with the Yankees. His name came up regarding steroids, and Pettit held a press conference. He admitted he used it. He described the scene when he was injured, was tired, and was trying to come back.

He knew other people were using them and just wanted to have the same competitive edge. He knew it was wrong, yet he did it anyway. He admitted his use, apologized for his actions, and swore he would not use them again. He was forgiven by the Yankees, the Yankee fans, and the baseball community. He will be remembered for his pitching days with the Yankees as well as his class and character during a time when he made a poor choice. People forgave Andy Pettit. So whether it's this story or another in history, make sure your child understands that it is usually the cover-up that's worse than the actual event.

SOCIAL & EMOTIONAL WELLNESS AND THE POWER OF RESILIENCY

> *Emotional intelligence is a way of recognizing, understanding, and choosing how we think, feel, and act. It shapes our interactions with others and our understanding of ourselves. It defines how and what we learn; it allows us to set priorities; it determines the majority of our daily actions. Research suggests it is responsible for as much as 80 percent of the "success" in our lives.*
>
> *— J. FREEDMAN, AUTHOR AND CEO OF SIX SECONDS*

What more can be said than in that quote? We strive for wellness in all areas for our children. This chapter explores different techniques and strategies to empower your child and strengthen their emotional wellness.

59. EMPOWER YOUR CHILDREN TO HANDLE THEIR BUSINESS.

If you take care of every little thing all the time, when and how will your children learn? Think about the world they are growing up in with Google, Alexa, and smartphones in hand. They have everything at their fingertips. Make them do the work themselves, such as making their lunches, their beds, their projects, and handling their conflicts. You certainly can be there with them and guide them, but if you make them do it, they will learn. They will be, if they are not already, on their own. Amazing, I have heard stories of parents contacting college professors about their kids' grades. Really? When do you cut the cord and let them figure it out, work it out? You can't fix everything, nor should you. Some of the best lessons are learned from handling one's own business.

60. Sometimes you just gotta stand up to it.

We want peace in our world and in our children's lives, and we never want them to resort to violence. Parents today are so quick to say, "My child is being bullied." When a parent says this to me, I ask a lot of questions: "What's led up to this? Has this happened before? With other children? What has your child done to try and prevent this?" These are the key questions. We want to empower our children to rise up and put an end to these types of situations. So what can we do? We can control what our child does for the most part, but we cannot control the actions of others. What can we teach our children to get through these situations? What tools can we give them? Start with these tips. If they have a conflict with another child and they do not like the way another child is treating them/speaking to them, try empowering them with some of these tools:

- Ignore the person/behavior.
- Tell them firmly to stop the behavior.
- Have them repeat it in a strong voice.
- Have them repeat it louder, firm voice, and with some mustard.
- Tell an adult or supervisor. I know there is an unwritten code of "snitches get stitches," but they have to tell a responsible adult. If the teachers do not know about it, they can't prevent it.
- If it still is happening, you bring it to the attention of the teacher. Preferably you meet with the teacher or Assistant Principal directly to speak about your concerns, but a phone call might work too, especially if you have already developed a relationship with the person.
- If they are being attacked physically, you have to teach your child to protect themselves. They are not a punching bag, and you can't allow them to get beat up without having the skills and confidence to properly defend themselves if they are being attacked or hit.

Hopefully, these types of things will never happen to your child, yet unfortunately, they do. You must empower your child to take action, or otherwise, it will continue. When your child does take action, they will feel more confident and be able to handle the next scenario that comes their way. Remember, this is a marathon, not a sprint. #Keeprolling

61. PART 2: DEALING WITH BULLYING

I rarely heard this word when I was in school. Did I know some kids were mean to other kids? YES. Were there fights? YES. Did kids say hurtful things to one another? YES. Yet, I never heard the word bully. On social media, our children are growing up with this concept, and it is at the forefront of their schooling experience. I will be frank on this topic. Empower your children. Strengthen your children. Give your children tools, topics, and techniques to manage the student that might say something harmful, make a comment, or give a dirty look regarding what sneakers children wear or the way their haircut looks. These things have happened from the beginning of time, yet somewhere the balance shifted from the parent and student responsibility to the schools' responsibility. Should the school be involved and help if there is a situation that does not stop? Yes, they absolutely should, but those steps are down the road.

So how can you empower them? Just like exercise, you have to train them. It is not a one-time antidote that you say here, do this, and there will never be any more bullying. Teach them to be confident, to act with confidence, and to learn what to say and what not to say when dealing with children who say and do hurtful things. This is an ongoing process and an ongoing journey, like many concepts in this book. Consistent conversations about how they are feeling, role-playing, giving them phrases to say, and body language to demonstrate their confident coping skills. I wrote about this topic a few times in this section, and some of the ideas and concepts overlap, yet I felt it important to keep them because I know this affects many kids out there. Keep doing your best for your kids. The results will show when they need it most!

62. GIVE THEM LINES FOR SELF-DEFENSE: ROLEPLAY, PRACTICE WITH THEM.

Jimmy is bothering me. No one sits with me at lunch. Joey bumped me in the hallway. Samantha gave me a dirty look. Michael wrote a nasty text about me. These are all real-life things that are going to happen to your children if they haven't already. I know the feeling. You want to grab them up and protect them from these shots from others. These continual pokes and prods by other kids continue to deflate your children, and it is upsetting to watch. But what to do? Should you swoop in and save them? Or do you want to empower them to handle their own battles and strengthen their inner coping skills? Surely it is the second and, the older they get, this should be easier for you to do. Empower them. Equip them. Roleplay with them. Practice with them what to do when "X" happens. What are some things that you could say, and what are some things that you could do?

My wife and I often work with the kids, roleplaying such situations. These situations are going to happen in schools. Firm voice, shoulders back, a stern look in the eye are just a few examples of things that we have practiced not only verbally but also in front of the mirror—just us, no one else around. It might seem silly in your child's bedroom, and you can even laugh about it, but when it happens in the hallway in that ninth-grade year, they will have some tools in their pocket ready to use. They will be prepared and comfortable because they have the words on the tip of the tongue.

Additionally, when these situations happen to us in real life—an angry shopper cut in front of us in line at a store or a waitress is less than respectful to us at a restaurant—we try to model the behavior that we want to see in our children. Remember, the apple doesn't fall far from the tree. If they see you speaking to a waitress that may be frustrated or rude to you and you turn around with some verbal judo and make a negative situation a positive one, you just gave your children another tool they can use.

63. TEST SCORES OR KINDNESS?

Which is more important? My advice: don't worry so much about their test scores or if your child is academically gifted, but do worry about if they sit with the kid who is alone in the cafeteria. See these two great social media posts below. The grades will be there, and their academics are very important, yet this trumps that. Being kind is something we need to model and talk to our kids about. How can they be kind to the kid in school that no one is friendly with? How can they demonstrate empathy towards others? What would you rather hear, that your kid got a 90 on a test or that they showed kindness towards someone?

WE NEED TO CARE LESS ABOUT WHETHER OUR CHILDREN ARE ACADEMICALLY GIFTED & MORE ABOUT WHETHER THEY SIT WITH THE LONELY KID IN THE CAFETERIA.

(Image from Pinterest)

I remember being in an assembly as a kid in school. The speaker was talking about bullying and the mean things kids can do. He shared the story of when he was walking home from school one day. He was quite down and had a terrible day. Some kids across the street were yelling at him and teasing him. He got startled and dropped his belongings. The kids across the street laughed and kept walking. A young man, not far behind him, stopped to help him and said to him, "Let it go. Those kids are dopey anyway."

They started talking as they walked. They shared a few things in common, and when they arrived at the young man's house, he asked the speaker if he wanted to play cards on the stoop. They played, and laughed, and enjoyed the time. The speaker even phoned home and asked if he could stay for dinner at the young man's house.

The speaker shared that the two went on to become very good friends and remained so for a long time. He continued that he valued that friend so much because, on that day, when he was walking home by himself and the kids were heckling him, he actually was going to kill himself. He felt that kids were cruel, and no one liked him. He was really depressed, and that one simple act of kindness and compassion from his friend saved him. The auditorium was speechless, and I remember that silence and the message sinking into everyone around me. Just a beautiful moment to see so many people learning and absorbing what kindness really can mean to someone who receives it.

So I ask once again, do you want your kid to get that 90 percent, or be the one helping the kid up with their belongings? They can be both.

64. KNOW YOUR KIDS' FRIENDS.

There is no secret recipe here. There is no easy formula. This one is straightforward and simple. Do whatever you have to do to get to know your kids' friends. These kids will be some of the most influential people for your children from the early ages of seven and eight through their teenage years. Invite them to your home. Meet their parents. Offer to drive them to the movies and even pick them up. Invite them over or on a camping trip where there's no cell phone reception where you can have meaningful conversations around a campfire or casting a fishing line. Take them for ice cream or go for a walk after dinner with them and their friends. These are all little things that you could do to get to know your children's friends. It is of the utmost importance.

If your child is at their home playing, how do they reprimand your children if they do something against the house rules? These are all things that you should be aware of and concerned about. Just because you have a polite conversation with someone after a school function doesn't mean your children should be able to sleep at their house without having further information. Your responsibility is not to judge others and their parenting style, but you are the sole person responsible for your children's safety. While you want to let your children figure it out on their own, you certainly want to have an idea of who these children are and who their parents are. Do they smoke in the house? Do they use drugs recreationally? Do they have alcohol readily available? Do they curse in front of your children?

These are all things that you should be aware of as the parent of YOUR child. It is not your business about the lifestyle or choices of other parents, yet it is your concern about who your child hangs out with and the influence that person may have on your kid.

65. FOCUS ON THEIR STRENGTHS, AND CHALLENGE THEIR WEAKNESSES.

Your child is beautiful. Your child is special. Your child is talented. I know this about kids, and I know parents believe this of their own children. Develop and enhance the things in which your children excel. Give them opportunities and let them run with them. If they continue and are enjoying a specific musical instrument or art project, give them another opportunity. See if they continue with it. Excellence is built on a spark followed by repetition and opportunity. Continue to expose your child to different experiences, places, and people. When there is something that they really enjoy or they really like, continue to expose your children to these opportunities.

When I was a young child, I fell in love with basketball. I loved the speed of the game, the *me versus you* mindset, and the physicality of it all. I loved the bounce of the ball, the smell of the gym, and the squeak of the sneakers. I knew this early and continued to play. My parents allowed me to and paid for me to attend summer camp, and I continued to excel. I went to sleepaway camp, and they even got me a hoop at the house. I remember playing countless hours in the front yard shooting hoops with my friends and family.

My freshman year in high school, my parents sent me to the top school in Brooklyn across the river from Staten Island, Xaverian High School for boys. They had a tremendous academic reputation as well as a historic basketball program. The great Chris Mullin, who starred at St. John's (NY), the Golden State Warriors, and was a member of the first Dream Team in the Olympics, is one of the most famous basketball alumni. I remember trying out for the freshman team, and there were 100 boys there for 12 spots. I was determined, focused, and relentless and did, indeed, make the team. I went on to play for years at Xaverian and continued on to Guilford College, playing hoops all the way. These experiences then lead to an officiating career, including earning a spot on the ACC officiating roster. Going back to the beginning of the story, the initial spark of interest, followed by repeated opportunities given to me by my parents, enriched my life. Enhance your children's strengths by creating opportunities for them and encouraging them in those areas.

66. SPEAK TO THEM OFTEN ABOUT SEXUALITY.

Our children are growing up in a very different world than we did. News and pop-culture discussions very much talk about sexuality and healthy sexual relationships much earlier than when we were children. Sexual assault, sexual aggressiveness, and abuse of power issues are at the forefront of people's lives today. Have conversations early and often with your children about sexuality. My experience in attending Guilford College, a small Quaker College in Greensboro, North Carolina, opened my understanding of different perspectives of sexuality and tolerant acceptance of others.

I attended a strict Catholic elementary school. Uniforms and uniformity and then went on to an all-boys Catholic high school. Again, uniforms, dress codes, and strictness. When I arrived at Guilford, it was a total culture swing. It was really the first experience I had seen of same-sex couples, who were quite open about it. What was nice about Guilford and the Quaker way is that all are accepted. It was calming to be in this type of culture where all are accepted.

Takeaway: Talk with your children about sexuality, early and often. They will see and hear things much earlier than we did. Have them have some understanding of all that is out there in today's world. Teach them empathy, understanding, compassion, and not to judge others just because they or their family makeup might look different than you or your family.

67. HAVE THEM JOIN A SERVICE ORGANIZATION.

Habitat for Humanity, the Food Pantry, the Scouts, Meals on Wheels, or whatever it is, get your kids involved in helping others early and often. Providing service to others and helping those less fortunate is an amazing experience not only for kids but also for adults. It provides a purpose, gives a sense of belonging, and truly warms the heart. Empathy and compassion for others are amazing for both parties, the giver and receiver, and when learned early, will be embedded in a child for a lifetime.

As a young child, I watched my parents be heavily involved in the community. My dad was the Community Board Chairman in Staten Island, New York, where he was constantly at meetings, public sessions, and in the newspaper advocating for services for the poor and the public. We also were heavily involved in our food pantry at the church.

After my dad passed away, they actually named the food pantry after him. My dad and my Aunt Maryann Bollinger were on-site packing bags, accepting food deliveries, and helping to manage the people each week. My mother was behind the scenes ordering the food, getting the grants, and making sure their certifications were up to date with New York City. I watched these behaviors by my parents, and, sure enough, here we are in our community in northeast Pennsylvania, involved in our local food pantry. Even though I was only 10- and 11-years old working with my dad at the pantry on Saturday mornings, I learned that it was important to help others.

Another great experience I had as a child is when NYC Mayor Michael Bloomberg donated one million trees to be planted in New York City. Each of the five boroughs of NYC was allotted a certain number of trees, and in our district, my dad was responsible for determining the locations where the trees were to be planted. All we had to do was provide the locations for the New York City Department of Parks and Recreation, and they would plant the trees. So each week, my dad and I would drive our car to a certain area, park, and get some extra exercise together. We would walk the streets of Staten Island, find the sites on the sidewalks that had no trees, and then submit the numbers of the corresponding home or property to the parks department. Here I am, 25 years later, bringing my kids to Staten Island to visit their grandmother and looking at all the trees that we were a part of planting to provide beauty and, equally importantly, oxygen to the citizens of New York City. I fondly remember these times with my dad. Get involved in service projects with your children.

68. GRANT ME THE WISDOM TO BE A DECISION-MAKER AND THE WORDS TO BE A COMMUNICATOR.

By Kevin Spainhour

Husband, Father, Coach, Teacher, and Principal from King, NC. (Kevin authored points 68 and 69)

We live in a parenting generation full of instructional how-to guides on the necessary steps to be a successful parent. Parenting 101 seminars are available for mothers and fathers from birth to post-adolescence. And yet, as a school administrator, I continue to interact with students in our schools who are in desperate need of stable, supportive parental guidance. Many children live in dysfunctional settings, left way too long and much too early to their own devices, or just lack proper role models in their lives. In these scenarios, the child's academic, social, and emotional development suffers. Even for the child being raised in a nuclear family, the lines are often blurred between quality parenting and the desire to forge a mutual friendship with its own distinct challenges.

Routine days are few and far between in the life of a school administrator. As with any job, the commute to work offers time to mentally prepare for the day. Being only seven minutes door-to-door doesn't exactly allow for much preparation on my daily commute. Therefore, I began saying a short little prayer every day on the way to work over five years ago to help clear my mind, set the tone for my day, and create a routine in a job that is anything but.

If you are religious, here is a short prayer you can say on your commute:

"God, grant me the wisdom to be a decision-maker and the words to be a communicator."

69. REASONS TO CRY: GUIDELINES TO GAUGE AUTHENTIC CHILDREN RESPONSES.

When I first heard about this next tip, I thought it was a little harsh and restricting. Kids need to release their emotions, right? Yet, when I saw it in action and tried it with my own children, it was actually masterful. Kevin Spainhour and his wife Laura developed the following as reasons when it was ok cry for their children. To respond to unnecessary crying and whining, they shared with their kids: "That's not a reason to cry!" Their kids would think about it for a moment and then stop crying because it wasn't a reason to cry.

This strategy stops senseless crying for the sake of crying or whining. It also defines the appropriate reasons spreading through a wide range of emotions. Here they are below. I urge you to give it a try!

- Hurt - physical pain: if you see blood, we understand
- Sad - emotional pain: if your dog dies, we understand
- Scared - uncertain or afraid: if you are lost in a store, we understand
- Overjoyed - emotional celebration: if Santa brings all your Christmas wishes, we understand

—*Kevin and Laura Spainhour*

70. ACCORDING TO JERRY SEINFELD, PARENTS ARE GIVING CHILDREN THE POISON P'S.

- **PR**AISE: Too much & too often
- **PL**EASURE: Too brand new & too much name brand
- **PR**OBLEM DISSOLVING: Fix-it attitude and failure prevention

Are we doing too much for our children? Do we swoop in too fast to save them or try to fix something for them because we don't want to see them struggle or suffer? Were our parents just tougher? Smarter? Or did they have just enough wisdom to know to let us be and let us figure it out? I can remember vividly (and I can't remember anything...Got CRS: Can't Remember Stuff!) so many different experiences where my parents did NOT rescue or made me work it out: played poorly or selfishly in a game; silence on the way home, followed by conversation. Getting handed a quarter before going out. I'd ask: what's this for?

My dad would respond, "For you to call someone else if you get in trouble. I'm not coming to get you." Getting my name in the paper for an accomplishment, and the response would be, "That paper will be on the bottom of someone's birdcage tomorrow covered in you know what." One of my favorites was working for my folks. Instead of hiring a contractor to repair the wall, paint the room, or build the deck, they hired me and paid me to figure it out. This was before YouTube or any of that, yet they had the patience to wait and watch me struggle to learn...all the while teaching me life lessons. Take-a-way: don't be so quick to swoop in and save the day. Let them be. Resilience and "bounce-back-ability" doesn't come in the form of a pill or injection. It builds up over time and through up and down experiences.

71. BLUEBIRD PARENTING.

by Dan Rockwell, the Leadership Freak
I read about this concept from Dan Rockwell's Leadership Freak blog. I love the concept, and my wife and I try to follow it in the very many scenarios that parents face. This is the blog from Dan with permission. Enjoy!

Surprisingly, baby bluebirds grow from birth to fledglings in about three weeks. Before they fledge, they require constant care and feeding. Eventually, they peek at the world through the small round door in their home.

Parents fly to the door with grubs and bugs. We hear the young going nuts. But at the fledging time, mom and dad shift tactics.

No food: Bluebird parents land at the door WITHOUT food at fledging time. We still hear crazy chirping, but the parent pauses and flies away. Eventually, daddy bluebird perches nearby with a juicy meal dangling from his beak. While daddy coaxes the young from the white birch, mommy demonstrates the desired behavior. Over and over, she flies from the birch to the house and back to where daddy dangles the bug.

Redefining help: Bluebirds expect their young to come to them. They stop showing up with food and expect their young to come and get it. Redefine 'help' when others are ALMOST ready to take flight.

Change your patterns of helping to instigate growth in others. It might be stressful, but it won't be disappointing if everyone knows why you stopped showing up with food.

Maybe you've been showing up in someone's office to check-in. Now it's time for them to show up in your office, for example. You change first. Help to a novice is an insult to experience.

If you don't change the way you help, others will eventually reject you. If you treat your teen like an infant, they will eventually hate you. Help differently, not necessarily help less. But if you expect to take on new challenges, eventually, you will help less.

I thank Dan for this excerpt, his leadership, and his excellent work. Check it out at LeadershipFreak.blog

72. FACE YOUR FEARS.

by Suzanne Carbonaro, my sister
Suzanne is an education professional, college professor, and extreme
NY Yankee fan. She is also Director of Academic Partnerships at
AEFIS in Philadelphia, PA. She was like my second mom, in a way,
my coach, and my protector. She always looked out for me. (She still
does!) Follow her on Twitter @suzieprof.

When I was around seven, I developed a fear of dying. There were several incidences at the root of this fear, but there is one in particular that I carry with me today as a reminder that we are stronger than we think we are, and with grit and commitment, we can overcome anything. I went to a pool party hosted by a friend who had a fancy house and was very popular at my school. I had never really been in an in-ground pool outside of maybe a kids' pool at a hotel with my parents and sister. I didn't realize that the rope and buoys in the pool separated the deep end from the shallow, and if I slipped slightly, the concrete sloped downward. This happened because about 25 kids were splashing and fooling around, and I went under and couldn't get above the water.

Eventually, people noticed, and I was lifted out of the pool. I remember the day and the incident clearly. I felt out of control, embarrassed, and scared. My parents came and picked me up, and I was safe, but the incident lived on throughout second grade.

I met with a psychologist, counselor, my teacher, and nothing seemed to ease my fears. Instead of my parents saying, "It's going to be okay," they gave me tough love and reminded me that life is precious, and we needed to live for today, conquer our fears, and never give up. So, when more invitations to pool parties came in the spring and summer months, they made me go. I didn't want anything to do with water, but I went because they told me I had to go. And I was resentful, but my mother did something for me that I carry with me even today. She didn't make me feel bad about being upset and fearful of the water; she signed me up for swimming lessons along with my siblings and my cousins. I didn't feel isolated or different because we did this together, which helped me grow stronger both mentally and physically. Feeling isolated was the worst part of the experience. Everyone else at the house pool parties could swim and were confident and excited in the water. So besides not knowing how to swim and fearing the water, I felt alone. She also taught me other self-soothing skills, such as how to control my breathing when I was anxious and how to talk to kids who made fun of me when I didn't feel comfortable near the water. These seem like simple concepts, but to a seven-year-old kid, they were the golden ticket to resilience. And by the end of that summer, I was taking advanced swimming, jumping off 20-foot diving boards, and riding in waves on the beaches of Long Island. If my parents had not given me that dose of tough love, sent me back out there to face my fears head-on, and taught me tools to survive and thrive, I wouldn't be running marathons, changing careers, and stepping out of my comfort zone to do what is right, not what is easiest today. Do I love the water today? Not really, but I do enjoy it, and I appreciate what this experience and my parents, particularly my mom, did for me—teaching me that I am stronger than I think I am.

—*Suzanne Carbonaro*

73. HOW CAN I HELP YOU? VS. WHAT DO YOU WANT?

This may sound like a simple command, yet it is a great mindset of leadership. Most people have a WIIFM mentality in life: *what's in it for me?* It's never too late to start talking about this matter and demonstrating for your children that " How can I help you?" is much more important than, "What's in it for me?" Helping and giving to others without expecting anything back is important for children (and, unfortunately, some adults). Model these behaviors and train them to ask the question: "How can I help?" You can never go wrong with that one!

74. SHAKE IT OFF AND STEP UP.

There once was an old donkey on a farm in the Midwest. One afternoon, the donkey was wandering around and fell down into an abandoned well. Smashing onto the floor and barely able to stand because of the narrow walls, the donkey began to wail. Frightened and scared, the donkey was hurt and could not move. The farmers and workers on the farm heard this awful screaming and wandered about until they eventually found the opening to the well and saw the donkey many feet below. The head farmer discussed with some of the workers what could be done. After some back-and-forth, they just decided that the old donkey should be put out of his misery the best way they could. Fill in the hole and eventually, the donkey would suffocate and die. So the workers began to shovel dirt into the old well. The donkey began to scream louder as the dirt started to pile upon him. With each shovelful, the donkey screamed once again until eventually, they did not hear any more noise. They assumed that the donkey had been covered and was quickly dying. They began to shovel more dirt. Then they heard a noise and saw the donkey about halfway up the hole.

Stunned, they looked down and realized what the donkey was doing. With each shovelful of dirt, the donkey was shaking it off and stepping up—another shovelful and another shake off of the dirt. They were shocked and overjoyed that the donkey took this awful situation and found a way out. They continued to shovel until eventually the donkey got to the top of the hole and was able to pull himself out.

Your child is going to fall. Your child is going to have dirt thrown on him, maybe literally and maybe figuratively. Teach your child to shake it off and step up. Life is not always about what happens to you, but more about how you react to it. Think about your life and all of the things that have happened to you. How many times have you shaken it off and stepped up? Teach your child to do the same and share this story with them. They will remember it the next time they fall down. Hopefully, it will not be into a deep well!

75. PLANNING FOR THE FUTURE

by Jenn Marotta

Parenting is the richest and most challenging experience of my life. I view it as a duty that I fulfill with all my love. When I say "duty," I mean that it is the single, greatest responsibility of my life. I have always tried to balance being in the present in the moment while keeping a constant eye on their futures...their future selves. Since they were just starting grade school, I've told my children that it is my responsibility to take care of them now, but we must prepare and plan for their future selves. I've said--- "I am looking at the 8-year-old you are now, but I am also planning how actions now will impact the 28-year-old you.".

I remember I was feeding my eldest in the high chair when she was around seven months old. I was talking to her... repeating words like "more, please, mmmm, thank you." At that time, we had some people visiting us, and a friend asked flippantly why I was talking to my child and asking her questions since she could not possibly answer me back. I was saddened that the person did not understand that we, as parents, need to keep our eye on what's next for our child. I knew I was speaking and asking questions to prepare her for when she was able to speak.

I view all our daily habits through that same lens. Chores, schedules, habits, and manners are all very molding. Life is in the details. It's conditioning. My children have encountered frustrations and failures in many small doses, thus building their "immune system" for future ones. They are a part of life, and it is our responsibility to prepare our children for them. I pray they continue to build their stamina to these aspects of life. Their success and happiness will be measured on how they react and plan around these events. All this may seem a bit calculated, but all the things you do for your children are driven by love, and they feel it because love is action, love is the follow-through, love is consistent, and love is modeled.

—*Jennifer Marotta*

76. DO YOU WANT TO GO IN?

January 1995: Guilford College men's basketball vs. Virginia Wesleyan University near Norfolk, Virginia. I was a sophomore, and we were getting beaten by 40 points in the second half, totally humiliated. My coaches were frustrated, and nothing was going right. There were about three minutes left in the game, and the coach came near the end of the bench where I was firmly planted. He asked two guys in front of me, upperclassmen, if they wanted to be put in the game. They both shook their heads no. He came to me, the last kid on the bench, and asked the same question. I leaped up like a firecracker and exclaimed, "Absolutely!" I got into the game like I was on fire. Got a rebound, hit a 3-pointer, and took a charge all in under three minutes. This was midway through my sophomore season, and I believe it changed the course of the rest of my playing career at Guilford. No longer was I the last kid on the bench, but someone who might get into the game even if it wasn't a blowout. I also felt I moved up the respect level with my coach. Regardless of the score or outcome of the game, I was ready to go in and do my best. I don't remember much from my playing days, but I remember that incident. I also remember the two young men who declined to go in and how their seasons spiraled after that moment. I'm not sure if they saw the floor again the remainder of the season. As I wrote in the first tip in this book, parenting, sports, and most things are more like a marathon or a marriage: a long journey with many ups and downs, good times, and bad times. Urge your children to consistently put their best foot forward at all times, but especially in the bad ones. It's easy to be a good teammate or player when things are going your way, and everyone is winning, but it's when the chips are down that true character is revealed.

77. DANCING ON STAGE: LEADERSHIP IN ALL FORMS

Here's another story from my time at Guilford College. This one is about my friends, Kevin and Laura Spainhour, who shared tips 69 and 70 earlier in the book. Sophomore year at Guilford, and an-up-and-coming band, Vertical Horizon, was playing in the auditorium at Guilford. We had seen them a couple of times at a local bar in Winston Salem, NC, and now they were at our school! It was very exciting. The concert was rocking, and we were having a blast. The band slowed it down and began to play "Sunrays and Saturdays" on stage.

The crowd began to slowly sway to the music, and all of a sudden,

Kevin grabbed Laura's hand and pulled her up on stage. They began to dance right next to the lead singer of the group! Wow! The crowd roared when they started dancing, and it was a beautiful moment. It is frozen in my memory. Shortly afterward, more couples started to go up and, soon, the whole stage was filled with students. It was one of those memories you have that are frozen in time, embedded in your memory bank. All because Kevin wasn't afraid to lead, not afraid to show his affection for his future wife, nor afraid to take a chance.

Let's teach our kids to take these leadership leaps. There really were not a lot of risks, just a spontaneous "let's do this." He broke the ice and took the leap paving the way for others to follow. It was a simple act, yet it was very telling of Kevin's confidence and leadership. Let's not only teach our children to create these experiences; let's model them as well.

BE INVOLVED & ENGAGED

> " *At the end of the day, the most overwhelming key to a child's success is the positive involvement of parents.* "
>
> — *JANE D. HULL, POLITICIAN AND EDUCATOR*

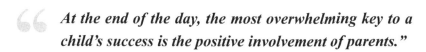

This can be a challenge for many of us. How do we balance all the obligations of our lives as adults and parents, yet engage in the lives of our children? Even in writing this book, I struggled to create the time to complete this project because I wanted to be there for my kids. In these points in this chapter, you will find tips to assist you in this journey.

78. THE MOST IMPORTANT NINE MINUTES OF THE DAY

The first three minutes when your children wake up, the first three minutes when they come home from school, and the last three minutes before they go to bed are the most important moments of your kids' day. If you focus greatly on these nine minutes, you will get great investment on your return. I read this concept online from a member of my #PLN (Professional Learning Network) years ago and loved it. Think about it; all that you can do in those nine minutes. Hugs, positive reinforcement, schedule check, organization help, ask questions, putting them in the right direction, positive thoughts, and again more hugs. Unfortunately, as a high school principal, I missed a lot of the first six minutes. During my days as a college basketball official, I missed many of the last three as well. I know I can't be at everything, but when I am home for one or all of those three minutes, I focus on making them the best they can be.

I'll share a second story from the great Bruce Springsteen's book entitled *Born to Run* (2017). It was a tremendous insight into Bruce's story. The aspect I found particularly interesting was when his kids were young. Bruce would have a gig and be out late into the evening and sleep until one or two in the afternoon. He came down one afternoon, his kids playing and running around the house, and his wife yelled at him that he was missing their childhood. She challenged him to get up when they got up because morning time and breakfast were the most important times of the day.

Bruce responded, and the next day, and for many after, Bruce became the breakfast guy in the morning. He would wake up when the kids did, greeted his children, and became invested and engaged in their lives, all starting with breakfast. Did it really fit his lifestyle? No, it did not, yet Bruce made that investment, which changed the course of his relationship with his children.

We are all very busy, and if your kids are between the ages of 8 and 18, you know how busy you are with your children. Try to slow down the express train and steal those minutes with your children. They are important times, and before long, those kids will be off in college, working, married, and starting their own family. #9Minutes. You'll be happy you did.

79. GO TO THE SCHOOL EVENTS.

Another play, another concert, another parent-teacher meeting. Kids that are involved and invested in school do better at school. The same goes for parents. Be involved in your kids' school. Go to their events. They only have one childhood. You are not only supporting them in their endeavors, but you are also building relationships with school staff. If the teacher and/or the administration can identify you by your name because they've seen you so often, that is a good thing. Volunteer for things and get involved.

There are so many opportunities and benefits to being involved in your child's school. While we're all tired on a weeknight after work and might be looking forward to some downtime either on a Friday night or weekend, take the time to volunteer and be involved. Maybe you're not good at arts and crafts, but maybe you could bring the supplies one day or even just encourage the kids not to leave the event. Your presence there is important not only to your child but in building relationships with the school staff. Most times, you get out of it what you put into it. #Investedparent

80. GIVE THEM SOME LEEWAY, YET NOT TOO MUCH.

How do you start doing this? How do you leave them home alone for the first time? Cell phone for the first time? Date for the first time? Drive, fly, go to college, cook, camp, swim, etc., etc. OMG, there are so many firsts for your kid(s). Scary, right? This is a tricky one because everyone is different: each family, each child, each school, the area where they live, etc. One family might have a kid walking home from the bus for the first time on their own. They live two blocks from the stop on a busy, well-lit street with friendly neighbors all around. Another family might have a very similar kid yet live 1.5 miles from the bus stop on a less crowded street with four unoccupied homes, no lights, and not a lot of traffic. See the difference? The point is you have to make the best decision for you and your child despite what others might be doing. Your scenario may be different, and your child may have a different comfort level. Continue to evaluate your situation and make the best decisions for your family. You'll know it. You'll feel it. Do the best you can and forget the rest.

I can remember my dad telling me to just do my best after my oldest, Claire, was born. He said people will give you all kinds of advice, some very strongly, but he told me to trust my gut, communicate excessively with my wife, and make each decision based on all of the factors around you doing what's best for your child.

So when starting out with new situations, give some leeway and go slow. Each time your child does well, you can give a little more. Even have a discussion with them about making smart choices, and if this goes well, maybe next time you can extend a little further or give a little more. #alittleatatime!

81. THE VILLAGE IS HOME.

by Genny Cornell

Genny is a mom, wife, and Chief Operating Officer of a local invest-ment firm in Milford, PA. She has an electric personality, a dynamic smile, and a big heart.

I met Genny through Port Jervis HS (NY) as she was a parent, and I was the Assistant Principal at the high school. After the first freshmen orientation for her son Sean, she reached out a few days later and shared with me, "Mr. Marotta, I need more. That orientation was just not enough for me." She was respectful and patient, yet persistent. Genny and I went on to become friends as her children grew up through the school and she ran the Parent-Teacher-Student-Associa-tion (PTSA) organization. She was helpful, organized, and really did some great things through the PTSA for the school and community. I was thrilled for her to share some parenting thoughts in the book. Enjoy!

They say, "It takes a village," and they are correct! However, they forget to mention, the heart of the village is HOME! Parenting for me started with my husband and I debating who's gonna change the dirty diaper, right down to who's picking them up from after-school practice! As school begins for children, it is an exciting time and yet can be terrifying when that first day comes. I always stressed to my children at a very young age, it's okay to be you. Be you, even if you are different from others, because that's what being an individual means!

Getting involved is key on all fronts...in your home, community, school, and job. I realized early on that school is one of the most important links to your child's interests, feelings, and behaviors. It's where they become independent and self-serving. Nightly at our dinner table, as a family, we discussed our day. All of us—my children knew what kind of day both mom and dad had, too. In middle school and all of high school, I stayed involved, particularly through our PTSA. This allowed me to engage in conversations proactively with Sean and Erin even if they said their day was "good."

I also embraced our school's technology. I was able to see what Sean and Erin were surrounded with daily from the district website. Social media, it can be a saving grace one day, and a weapon the next. I went out of my way to keep our kids from just "locking" themselves in their room and making the internet their home within our home. Sports helped a lot with that, as available downtime was not always an option for Sean or Erin.

No one is perfect, but when you speak from your heart, with conviction or sincerity, whichever may be needed, it displays the purest form of respect. Communication is priceless; always have an open ear, strong shoulder, and a warm heart when someone needs you to listen to them.

—*Genny Cornell*

82. YES, YOU ARE STILL GOING.

I was leaving my children's athletic contest once, and I heard a child near us telling his parents about the makeup game that was being scheduled because the original was canceled. The child told the parent about the date and time of the game and said it's really not that important because I'm not gonna play anyway. The parent agreed and said to the child that they did not have to go. In my mind, the music stopped, and the record screeched, and it was like a punch in the gut. What do you mean you're not going and it is ok just because you are not going to play? I was so turned off by this comment and that it was allowed to happen. When your children sign up for something (sports, music, camp, etc.), they make a commitment and should keep that commitment, even if they do not like it. If they choose they do not want to play that sport the next season or take that music class again next year, that is ok in my opinion. Our children are allowed to change their minds, yet when they commit to something, we should help them see these commitments through.

Two stories come to mind:

1. A student-athlete injured his knee the week before the last game, with no chance of playing, and was out for the remainder of the season, even if the team were to advance. I walked out on the field on Friday Night Lights, and standing on the sideline in full uniform on crutches was this young man. He was there waving the towel shoulder to shoulder with his teammates cheering them on. This went on for weeks as the team advanced in the playoffs. Kudos to this young man and his family for staying the course.

2. A star infielder for a high school softball team developed

an infection in her mouth and had to have her wisdom teeth pulled immediately. This was the morning of the big playoff game. Her father took her for the surgery, brought her home to rest for a few hours, then to the field to cheer on her teammates. She suited up not to play in the game but to be there for her team, jaws packed with gauze. I was blown away when I heard this story. Four wisdom teeth pulled in the morning and then in full uniform on the bench cheeks packed with ice. That's tough! Do you think she tells her kids that story now as a mother herself? You think her teammates remember if they got a hit that game or that their teammate was there no matter what? This story is pretty extreme, yet it certainly makes the point about making a commitment. Have your child stay the course and not take the easy road because they don't feel like it.

83. THE MAN IN THE ARENA

It is not the critic who counts; not the man who points out how the strong man stumbles, or where the doer of deeds could have done them better. The credit belongs to the man who is actually in the arena, whose face is marred by dust and sweat and blood; who strives valiantly; who errs, who comes short again and again, because there is no effort without error and shortcoming; but who does actually strive to do the deeds; who knows great enthusiasms, the great devotions; who spends himself in a worthy cause; who at the best knows, in the end, the triumph of high achievement, and who at the worst, if he fails, at least fails while daring greatly, so that his place shall never be with those cold and timid souls who neither know victory nor defeat.

— The Man in the Arena: April 23rd, 1910 Teddy Roosevelt

Your child will have many experiences along the way. Sometimes they are in the arena, and sometimes they are in the crowd. Have them be mindful of being critical of others. It is so easy sometimes: a ref misses a call, a teacher writes a grammatical mistake, a celebrity has an embarrassing arrest. Encourage your child to put themselves out there and "be in the arena" more often than sitting back and being the "pointer out of how the strong man stumbles." Being in the arena makes for an environment to be at your best when it matters most. It helps sharpen your saw and senses to know that eyes are on you and you have to perform.

There will be opportunities along the way: science fairs, singing a solo in a concert, presenting a program at a Board of Education meeting, or church hall function. Find the balance between pushing your child and creating opportunities where you are encouraging them to join. Maybe they're not ready, but continue to provide those opportunities for if and when they are ready.

As I write this book, my oldest daughter Claire is in her early teens. She has a beautiful voice and sings throughout the house and in our yard. Every time I turn around, she is singing a beautiful song. I want to record them and capture each one. I have encouraged her many times to try an open mic night, sing in the church choir, or even get on stage at a restaurant where a local singer may perform. She has yet to jump at these opportunities and has even gotten frustrated with me by continuing to ask her, so I walk that fine line of pushing and encouraging while giving her space. Will she jump in the arena one day? I don't know, and eventually, the decision will be hers, but I can recognize the talent. I would love to see her pursue singing, but if it is to be, it is up to me (her really), so I will continue to compliment her and support her in her love of singing and music.

84. BE INVOLVED AND ENGAGED.

by Frank Vogel

Frank is a husband and father in Milford, PA. He retired from the New Jersey State Parole Board and serves his family and his community in many facets. Always looking to help or pitch in, Frank is ready with a smile, joke, and laugh. In this excerpt, Frank shares the story of his family. The Vogels and our family became friends through church, and we quickly noticed that we shared a lot of the same values, including caring greatly for our children. Frank is a hardworking, friendly man who serves his family well.

Before my wife and I decided to have children, we discussed what type of parents we wanted to be and how to raise our children. We talked about the sacrifices we would make financially so we could be more involved in their lives. We decided that my wife would quit her job once we had children and become a stay-at-home mom. This put a strain on us financially, but we felt that this was in the best interest of our family. It would allow her to spend as much time as possible with our children, which included reading to them and teaching them the fundamentals of academics at such an important age. We also discussed how we wanted our children to have a strong faith base and to not only attend church regularly but to be involved in the church activities and masses. We also wanted to be involved in their extracurricular activities. My wife was a class parent, Girl Scout leader, and an officer in the Parent-Teacher-Student-Association (PTSA), just to mention a few examples. I would coach their teams in T-ball, soccer, etc. We both agreed that raising our children would take a combined effort, and we had to consistently communicate with each other.

Fortunately, after all our discussions about how we wanted to raise our children, we were blessed with three girls. Currently, they are 13, 15, and 17 years old and, though it has been a challenge, it has been so fulfilling. My wife and I know we are blessed and have tried to stay with our original plan in raising children, which seems to be working. Even though there have been some bumps in the road, I could not be more proud of how these three young ladies have grown in this short period.

We feel that communication with our children, though it seems like common sense, is such an important part of raising children. Since we are so busy, we go through phases where we don't get to have dinner as a family every night. So, the times that we do get to sit down together and have a meal are a great time to catch up and talk about our day or anything on our minds. We also talk in the car or when we are all getting ready in the morning.

One topic I talk about often with my kids is the negative effects of drugs and alcohol. Before I retired, I was a New Jersey State Parole Officer, and many of my cases involved substance abuse. Without giving details, my children received an education on how substance abuse can damage so many lives and destroy families. Drugs and alcohol exposure is one of my biggest fears as a parent, and I can only hope that the conversations that we had and continue to have will help my children make the right decisions if ever exposed to these substances.

—*Frank Vogel*

85. FAMILY GAME NIGHTS

Set dates to have family game nights. There are just so many positives that come from this; so many memories are created. Think about your junk closet. How many board games do you actually have in there? PLAY THEM! And make the time to do it. Your kids will thank you, and it will be good for you. At that moment, no chores, no bickering, no phones, no nothing: just family time, just quality time. You can rotate who gets to make the selection and, if time is tight, even set a timer to end the game, not necessarily when it is over, but when the timer goes off. A few of our family favorites are Spinners, Apples to Apples, Scrabble, Family Challenge, and even though it takes a long time--Monopoly. Our son Matthew still loves it, and he will take your money! No breaks on rent either! #familygamenight!

86. CELL PHONE-FREE ZONES

Create cell phone-free zones in the house. You are busy, your kids are busy, yet have some spots that are cell phone free. While our kids are still young, one rule that we have is that our kids do NOT charge their phones in their rooms at night. The temptation to look at the phone or hear those notifications are just too great. This will also create disrupted sleep, which is so detrimental to the health and wellness of your child (Haas, 2018).

Another spot we have is at the dinner table. No phones at or near the dinner table, especially during dinner. This is a sacred time. As kids when the phone rang, my mom and dad would say leave it, and they would have to call back. They did NOT want dinner interrupted, and here now, in our home, my wife and I do the same. 20, 25 mins a day, no phones, no interruptions—just dinner time, just talking time with the family.

Another culture builder you can do in your house is to create cell phone bans for certain times, certain events. Not everyone believes in these same philosophies, and when you have gatherings, people may be on their phones at your dinner table or during a family game or event. Set the tone/expectation early and have a cell phone basket or have a conversation with folks about the atmosphere you are trying to create. One long tradition we have in our home is Camp Marotta. This is a long weekend, 4-5 day visits from family to our home in Milford, PA. We have played games, had campfires, gone hiking, slept in the yard, gone rafting, etc. All old-school summer camp-type activities.

As the "campers," as we called them (our nieces and nephews), started to get cell phones, we banned the electronics, so the kids would engage with one another and not be glued to the screen. We also only allowed one call per day to their parents, so they wouldn't be homesick and, once again, be engaged with the camp. It's been great for not only our immediate family, but also for our siblings, cousins, and their families too. We have a ton of great memories and are grateful for the times that we had with our family over those years.

Camp Marotta Pictures, Summer 2019

Both these pictures are from great times at Camp Marotta. The first is the walk to Grandma & Grandpa's (or Mima & Gwa-Gwa as they lovingly call them) in their camp sweat jackets. The second is us at a local lake. Paddleboarding, swimming, BBQing, playing, and just having good ol' summer fun.

*Sidenote: Like the famous Apple holiday commercial showing the "disengaged teen" who was actually documenting and editing family time on her phone, we started to allow the teens to take pics and videos to create cool digital memories of the camp experiences. The kids made some really awesome songs, memes, and tributes to the camp and their cousins. This is an example of adapting and changing your rules as you move forward.

87. SOMETIMES, JUST GET AWAY FROM IT.

I can remember the days as a kid just riding my bike around with no destination or just meeting up with my neighborhood friends and asking that magical question, "What do you guys want to do?" Our world is becoming more crowded and busy—calendars, school projects, part-time jobs, and more and more and more. My wife and I have had our kids tell us more than once, "Can we just be? And my answer has been, "And do what?" The answer has morphed into: let's find out and/or nothing. I am a planner and constantly schedule my time so I can be productive and make sure I am putting my time into the people/things that are most important. It has been my wife and kids that have helped slow me down to do just nothing. Have thumb-wrestles, cuddle, wonder, daydream, and just be in the moment with one another. I believe this is the reason that I love #snowdays. It creates 12-15 hours of unscheduled time that I make sure I do not clutter with unwanted items. This is where/when we can just get away from it: responsibilities, phones, schedules, and just have some nice family time making soup, playing games, playing in the snow, going to a local play place, etc.

My wife and I also plan little get-a-ways that literally help us "get away from it." A weekend at a hotel with a pool or at a family or friends' house. It doesn't have to be expensive or something extravagant, just time for you and your family to get away from the grind. These are amazing positive experiences where you are not fixing something in your house, looking at the bills that need to be paid, cooking dinner, or doing all of the daily tasks that fill our days (and have to be done!). These 24-48 hour get-a-ways deposit much-needed refueling in our hearts and minds.

We most recently looked on Airbnb for an "unplugged" place. A rental with no Wi-Fi or service. It has electricity yet off the grid. I have never done something like this, yet I am quite curious to try. Regardless of the spot (can even be a staycation—staying at home and making it a vacation), pick some times where you take your family to "get away from it all!"

DEVELOPING POSITIVE RELATIONSHIPS WITH SCHOOL STAFF

> *Positive relationships in schools are central to the well-being of both students and educators and the underpin of an effective learning environment."*
>
> *— SUE ROFFEY, AUTHOR AND DIRECTOR OF WELL-BEING AUSTRALIA*

While it will not be perfect all the time, and you may have concerns or problems at times, work at building your relationship with the schools and their personnel. Try not to overreact, don't believe everything you hear, and this is a marathon, not a sprint —all this and more in this chapter.

88. UPDATE YOUR INFORMATION.

Simple. Constantly update your info with the school. This is coming from someone who had the same phone number (yes, back in the day when there were only house phones) my whole life until I got married. This is not the case with many families, as in the cell phone age, people's information and numbers change. Make sure your information is correct at the school. It is amazing to me, as the Principal, how often this is NOT the case, where we are tracking down info from kids, other family members, or whomever we can to get in touch with the school. We have had situations at school where kids have gone to the emergency room, and I have been there late into the evening because I was not able to get in touch with a family member. #updateyourinfo

89. ASK FOR THEIR RECOMMENDATIONS.

Your child's educators and counselors are professionals. They have been trained for years and have years of experience working with children. Ask them what they think. Whatever the situation is, whether a conflict with another student, possible ADHD diagnosis, suspension for a fight, or college process, ask them what they think. You do not have to take their advice, but they might offer a suggestion or avenue that you haven't thought of before. It will also help build a stronger bond with that teacher, counselor, or administrator because you validate their position and professionalism at the school.

90. IF YOU HAVE CONNECTIONS, BRING THEM TO SCHOOL.

Does your neighbor work at the local track where racers come and race their cars? Is your cousin the local soda and beer distributor that could provide cases of water for an event? Is your son a backup on Broadway? Did your parents write for *The New York Times*? Any and all of these are things that could benefit kids and students. Reach out to your child's teacher and/or principal and offer to bring that guest or that connection to the school. Maybe you could get a morning at the movies before the main theaters open of the latest film that's coming out or a historical film that could benefit students in social studies classes because you know the manager at the local movie theater. There are so many times that resources free of charge can benefit schools and their kids. If you have connections, try to bring them into schools, and do not look for any favors in return. You should not expect that your child will be picked for the lead in the play or start on the basketball team because you work for Nike and were able to provide free uniforms. Do for the sake of doing and not so your kid receives preferential treatment. Do it to help kids.

91. GIVE YOUR NAME MULTIPLE TIMES WHEN YOU GREET PEOPLE AT THE SCHOOL.

You will be at your child's school often. The administrators and teachers see many, many people throughout the week. *Don't assume they remember your name.* Some educators have that uncanny ability to remember a name and face right away. Some others work really hard at it, and some, like me, repeat, repeat, and repeat names until memorized. When you arrive at that function, stick your hand out and say, "Hello Principal Smith, _____(insert your name), Timmy's dad/mom." Principal Smith might say, "Oh, yes, I knew that," yet they are probably saying to themselves, "I'm glad this awesome parent introduced themselves right away like that." I would say do this at least three times, if not four. If they haven't gotten it after four times, shame on them. They should have it down by then. Yet give them the benefit.

I know I am very conscious of people's names and work at it. How? I write it down on my pad I always have with me! It is good for all parties, especially your kid when the Principal/Teachers know the names and faces of your children. Most times, that same educator will touch base with the child the next day at school to share the encounter looping all parties back together. This is a powerful yet simple interaction that can go a long way in building relationships with the school and supporting your child, all because you kept giving your name and showing your face to the school staff.

92. DO NOT BE SO QUICK TO SAY, "NOT MY KID."

You are going to get a phone call that something happened. Your kid, at some point, will be involved in something, if they have not already, so hear the whole story. Before you blindly defend your child or the situation, hear from your child, hear from the teacher, hear from the school. Listen. Take a breath. Process. Reflect. Ask questions. Write a recount of the story. Sleep on it. Ask more questions. Pause. Talk with your spouse/significant other. You get the gist.

There are usually three sides to every story: your kid's, the other kid's, and the exact truth. The most egregious story of *Not my Kid* I remember in a situation like this is when we caught a student stealing money at a school event. The person who normally checks the money said it seemed a little short of what it normally is. She asked the kids who worked the event if anything was out of the ordinary, and they said no. She came to me next, so we went to the video camera. Sure enough, clear as day, on camera it showed the student sliding money away from the cash drawer in her hand, off the table, onto her lap, and then into her pocket. The student did this three times over the period of the event. Really good kid, really bad situation.

I met with the student, with the parent on the phone, and the mother claimed her daughter did not take the money. The mother wanted to know why I was accusing her child. I told her we are interviewing all the students, even though there was no evidence of the other kids doing anything wrong. I called the mom back and asked her to come in.

Our school policy is that we do not show parents our security camera for a variety of reasons. I told the mother I have her child on camera stealing the money three times. She said, "no way." I told her I would proceed with punishment, and she was livid, insisting that there was no way her child did what I was saying and that I must have something against the daughter. (Remember, when I wrote a few paragraphs up that many times parents look to blame someone or something when things go wrong?) Well, I decided I would bend the rules in this scenario and show the tape because it was so clear on film that the child took the money. I showed her the clip where the child stole the money, waiting for her to say something like, "OMG...I am so sorry, Mr. Marotta. I can't believe my child did this. I'll take care of it." Instead, she stared blankly at me and said, "What? I don't see anything." Shocked, I gave her a play-by-play as I showed it again, and she still argued with me. I ended our meeting because it was not going anywhere, handed down the discipline, and could not recoup the missing funds. The moral of the story is even when the school has 100% video evidence of a situation, there are those parents out there that still say, "NOT MY KID." Don't be that parent!

93. KNOW THE SCHOOL POLICIES AND RULES.

As your child goes through different grades, different schools, and different levels of their education, you and/or your spouse should stay involved and know the school policies. Know the history and know the how and why certain things are the way they are. As you go through and get to know staff and personnel, ask questions. How do kids get into honors classes? What is the punishment for vaping? Are the kids allowed to use their cell phones in class? Should they have their own Chromebook? Are they allowed to wear ripped jeans? All of these things are your responsibility to know, so if something happens, you're not caught off guard. You can help set the ground-work with your child and the school. Review the school handbook and the school website. Schools are usually mandated to post different things online, including policies and procedures like the code of conduct and transportation requirements. Read the notes that come home and be up to date on trends and schools.

94. DO NOT BASH TEACHERS OR ADMINISTRATORS ON SOCIAL MEDIA.

You will get frustrated. You will disagree. You will be unhappy with decisions made by teachers and administrators along the way. It's only natural and, just like anything in life, there are different opinions. Do not take your opinions to social media. This will only further damage your relationship with the school administration. Often, teachers and administrators get a raw deal in terms of people's opinions of them. They hear rumors, the local chat at the coffee shop, and things like that. I caution you to not put negative things about the school district on social media. Meet with the people and work with them head-on. Tell them your concerns or things that may cause you to be upset, but putting bad news or upset opinions on social media is not going to improve your situation or the issue that you are upset about. It will only make for more defense on the part of teachers, administrators, and the school district. People don't forget things like that. I've had many negative things written about me online and on social media, which hurts when they are not even true. For some reason, in our society today, people feel the need to express them-selves in this manner, and, as a high school principal, I am telling you this is not a good move. Hit pause, sleep on it, and do not post rants. Writing out your thoughts, even talking them out, is a good practice;

just do not post them on social media for all to see. Meet with the school and talk it out.

95. ASK NOT WHAT YOUR SCHOOL DISTRICT CAN DO FOR YOU; ASK WHAT YOU CAN DO FOR YOUR SCHOOL DISTRICT.

WIFM: what's in it for me? This can be the mindset of people and not just when they're talking about the school district that their children attend, but in many aspects of life. Certainly, we understand fully that you want the best for your child, and I believe it is our role to be a servant leader and not a doormat running around spoiling our students. Acting as a servant leader means acting with the mindset of how can I help you, how can I get you closer to your goals, and how can I help you become a better person and student? What is your mindset towards the school? Are there things that you can add and bring to the school district? Are you a parent volunteer that helps at different functions? In the lower grades, have you been a mystery reader, a parent that sponsored a lunch for the hundredth day of school? If you have the mindset of *how can I help* and *what can I do for the school*, this will shift your paradigm on things. It will help build relationships and get you more engaged in your child's education and the school district.

I have been fortunate in my life to grow in my positions of leadership as a husband, father, principal, community leader, as well as a former college basketball official. It has been fun along the way to be able to speak to the different athletic teams not only in my school district but in my neighboring school district where we live, Delaware Valley. I have been grateful to share my experiences on and off the court in the world of officiating with different camps, coaching seminars, and local referee organizations. Also, it has been a joy for me to officiate some local youth contests, three-on-three summer tourna-

ments, and community events like the Harlem Wizards, a local Globe-
trotter-like team that puts on a great show. This allows me to give
back to my school and community because of an experience outside
my role as a high school principal.

So on the K-12 journey that you are on with your children,
certainly expect the best and have them take every opportunity they
can to engage themselves, become better learners, and have tremendous experiences, but look for opportunities to ask the question,
"What can I do for the school district?"

96. THE APPLE DOESN'T FALL FAR FROM THE TREE.

We've had this many times in my office. Scenario: I call a parent to
discuss their child's lateness to school, and both the parent and the
child are late to the meeting. Scenario: I called a parent to tell them
their child is being suspended for cursing at a staff member, and they
tell me on the other line that this is F&^%$#% B&^*s$%^.

The apple doesn't fall far from the tree. Be aware of this and that
your children are going to take your positive and negative traits. Be
mindful of the behaviors that you display and the actions that you take
in front of your children. They will mirror these behaviors and
actions.

97. HELP YOUR CHILD MAKE THEIR GOALS CLEAR WITH THE SCHOOL COUNSELOR AND ALL STAKEHOLDERS.

Set a yearly meeting with the guidance counselor to discuss and share
about your child's goals and dreams. If your child wants to go into
one of the military academies, that must be brought up. If they want
to go into HVAC, that should be discussed. If they have an Individual
Education Plan (IEP) with specific items on it for your child's benefit,

be clear and bring it up. Don't assume that the counselors are aware of these things. Hopefully, they are because you have developed a relationship with the counselor, but a friendly reminder is ok. They have hundreds of students; you just have your child or children. You are not being pushy or 'in their face,' yet you are opening the door of communication with the school and specifically your child's counselor.

98. BE INVOLVED IN THE SCHEDULING PROCESS.

Once or twice a year (in the secondary grades), it will be time for your child to meet with their counselors to discuss and plan their classes for the next year. Each school is a bit different, but you should be part of the process—honors classes, elective classes, NCAA eligibility, technical programs, college, Advanced Placement courses, etc. Even if you are just there to represent your child and they do all the talking about their goals, interests, and classes for the future, it is a good thing if you are there. Your presence will take it up one notch for the counselor to make sure they have all their ducks in a row and are properly prepared for the parent/student meeting. Also, that is one more connection point you have with your child. There are a lot of these along the journey, so make sure that you can be there to help be part of your child's scheduling session.

99. GET TO KNOW THE GUIDANCE COUNSELOR.

A guidance counselor can be a very key person in your child's educational journey. They are the go-to for so many different things. On the elementary level, they are involved in character education, student conflicts, and social/emotional issues. If your child feels comfortable and knows who the counselor is, they will go to that person. On the secondary level, they are major factors in your child's scheduling of classes, SATs, and college prep standardized tests. In all things gearing towards your child's future, the guidance counselor is heavily involved. Develop a relationship with the counselor. Ensure they have your contact information and be part of the discussions in the journey with your child. Don't direct all the traffic, but be present and be part of the discussion. The guidance counselor could have a strong influence on your child as well. If they had a good experience at a certain college does impact how they speak to your child about a certain school or region. If many kids have been successful at a specific place, they might be more inclined to point your child in that school's direction.

Additionally, they will share the pluses and minuses of going to college close versus far away, a big school versus a small school, a two-year school versus a four-year school, and so much more. The point is, in short, to make a connection with the guidance counselor and make sure they know who you are and who your child is.

100. THE NEW KID

Written by Julie Balogh, parent and Guidance Counselor at Port Jervis High School

"The new kid." A phrase that was often used about me. From third grade to senior year, I attended five school districts and lived in eight different homes in three different states (NY, FL, CO.) After age seven, the longest I ever lived at an address was just under two years. At the pinnacle of relocating, I attended five different schools in four years.

There are many reasons why children move to different schools. Thankfully, my reasoning was due to my father getting transferred within his career with IBM. (IBM is an acronym for International Business Machines OR "I've Been Moved.") Other reasons that children change schools are military moves, in search of affordable housing, homelessness, child protection placement, runaways, migrant workers, divorce, foster care/adoption, or like me: parental career moves. Note: children rarely, if ever, WANT to move—it is not usually a child's choice to change schools, uproot their life, make new friends, and leave their old friends/neighborhood. It is a true test of resilience.

Moving is one of the most stressful things a family can go through. Research shows that moving is cited as being even more stressful than divorce. Children usually have absolutely no control over the decisions associated with moving or the relocation process, which can compound the stress they feel.

Entering a new school for the first time is an unexplainable feeling. Feeling overwhelmed is an understatement; butterflies in the stomach feel like pterodactyls on double espressos. I remember these feelings vividly. I also have built a tolerance to change. After relocating a couple of times, I learned that things get easier each day. Smiling was something that got me through a lot of situations—albeit often a forced smile, it usually worked. I would smile at people until they smiled in return. It was difficult to get involved with school activities since I felt that the students were already established in their groups. I often stuck with individual-based sports like gymnastics, tennis, and diving. Large groups of interdependent people were not my thing. I was very self-reliant outside of my immediate family. Luckily enough, I grew up with strong connections within my family unit—something not all children have.

As a school counselor, I often utilize my past experiences when working with "new" students. Before they even set foot in the building, I like the opportunity to talk with them on the phone and then email their teachers a background on them. One teacher, in particular, has compared my introduction emails to singles ads. I introduce the student by name, where they are from, their interests, who they live with, and what lunchtime they have. When I meet with the student for the first time, I smile a lot—even if they don't return the gesture. I try not to be too quick or overwhelming because I know the pterodactyls in their stomach are wreaking havoc. I stick to the basics on the first day: where they need to be and when, how to get around the building, and how to order lunch. I introduce the students to key people: hall monitors, clerical staff, cafeteria workers, administration, counselors, and their teachers. I show them the locker room and then assure them that there is no pool and no third floor—no matter what anyone says. We give them a map, a schedule, a listing of clubs and activities, and a planner. I go over simple rules about dress code and cell phone use. Other than that, they need to go and experience the day. They always find their resilience—either day one or day 20, they will figure out that every day gets a bit easier, and the pterodactyls turn to butterflies, and then the butterflies fly away completely.

Teachers play a huge role in the transition a student takes from "new" to "acclimated." Welcoming, accommodating gestures go a very long way when a student enters a classroom for the first time. It's like hosting a party that keeps getting bigger—you make room, order more food, and smile. Maybe, for future events, you whisper to your spouse —"let me know how many people you're inviting next time so that I'm not caught off guard." Regardless, you never turn away a guest at the door or make them feel unwelcome. If the class is not a good fit, that is a conversation between the teacher and the school counselor at another time. For the time being—we make room for "the new kid." Connections that a new student makes on the first day and during their daily schedule can make or break them.

I often tell new students that they have a "clean slate" when they start a new school—"No one knows you. You can reinvent yourself if you wish." Although their school record follows them, it is not advertised to the teachers or staff. I also caution students to take a breath before diving into a friendship with the first person who invites them to sit with them at lunch. They have choices… be aware of ALL the choices. Get to know people a little at a time each day. "Take a lap before you commit to a location" (Movie: Clueless, 1995).

I (Julie Balogh) have lived in my current home for 15 years— much longer than I have ever lived anywhere. My children have attended the same school district since kindergarten. It's amazing how things work out in different ways. I don't think I would be the outgoing, friendly, "multiplier" I am today if I hadn't honed my resilience and found my grit through relocation. I search for new, unknown people, places, and cultures for my children to experience and navigate since they do not have the option (yet) of relocating. Travel is a large part of our children's' upbringing, and the respect they have for various cultures (in or outside the US) is important to us as their parents. We want them to be "the new kid," the "outsider" once in a while. It cultivates relationships, resilience, and grit.

In short, relocating really can stink as a kid living through it. However, looking back—it made me who I am today. It also has helped me be a better School Counselor, parent, and traveler. For educators welcoming a new student: smile at the "new kid," make room at the party table, and be consistently welcoming—they are in shock the first few days, and it will take time for them to warm up. It's a lot like transplanting a plant... Moving even a healthy plant can damage roots and strain the plant. Plants often droop after transplant because of shock. Most plants usually recover and perk up after a few days of water and nourishment UNLESS, of course, they have been uprooted incorrectly or abruptly, previously malnourished, and/or replanted incorrectly. Keep in mind that children come from all types of backgrounds and family lives—you may never know exactly WHY they stepped foot into a new school.

COMMUNICATION

> *Communication is power. Those who have mastered its effective use can change their own experience of the world and the world's experience of them. All behaviors and feelings find their original roots in some form of communication.*"
>
> — *TONY ROBBINS*

W ork hard to develop your relationships with the schools. Don't overreact, don't believe everything you hear, and remember, from tip #1, it's a marathon, not a sprint. In this chapter, you will find tips and ways to increase and better your communication with the school. It is a two-way street, yet you have 100% control of your end, so do your best to grow those relationships.

101. DO NOT CALL FOR EVERYTHING.

Don't understand the homework assignment? Missed the spring fling dance due date? Forgot lunch at home? Kid allegedly said something not nice to your kid? All concerns. All minor irritants, yet you do not have to call for each one. Pick your spots when you call, so you do not become the parent who cries wolf and calls at the drop of a hat. So what can you do? A few things such as check-in with other parents or other kids about the homework. Call the homework hotline (if they have one.) Send in a note about the due date or, even better, have your child look into it. Let a day pass. See if the negative comment towards your kid just passes, and they shake it off. So many things could happen without that phone call about a minor issue. I am all for communication with parents and teachers, yet I challenge you to pick your issues. If you call each time something pops up and you do not let your kid handle it, you are taking away their ability to deal with situations, their problem-solving thinking cap. It will work out and call when you need to, not for each little thing.

102. ASK YOUR CHILD: DID YOU ASK A QUESTION TODAY?

Throughout time parents have asked, "How was school today?" Most times, the child will answer the same, "It was ok." If you keep asking the same question, you will keep getting the same answer. If you asked if they asked a question, you could get them to start thinking. I heard the quote, "Curiosity is emotional hunger." How can you cultivate curiosity in your children? Ask them questions. Ask them I wonder questions. And ask the question to them if they asked a question today. The brave student asks the question that many are hesitant to ask. So train them, urge them, and challenge them to ask questions.

You never know where the conversation will turn if they answer you YES that they did indeed ask a question vs. "how was school today?"

103. SIGN UP ELECTRONICALLY.

The world is ever-changing. I can remember going from my first tape cassette player to my first CD player. I can remember getting my first cell phone. I can remember the first time I sent an electronic check through my bank account. Facing all of these changes, I wasn't really nervous but felt more like jumping off a big diving board the first time into the pool. You know there's water at the bottom, and you just brace yourself for impact. Well, the same goes for new types of communication with your child's school, whether it is a new app or a new student management system. Electronic viewing of report cards? Interactive meetings with teachers? Whatever it is, sign up for it. You can still request an old-fashioned face-to-face meeting or phone call with the teacher, but the more avenues you are signed up to be connected with the school, the better off you are. Hopefully, your child's school is progressive and continues to advance these types of connections for parents.

As I am writing this section of the book today, I'm keeping my fingers crossed as principal because the school where I work is having its first electronics sign-ups for parent/ teacher conferences. Part of me is embarrassed that it took so long, yet the other part of me is keeping my fingers crossed that it goes well and parents actually use it. (Update--it went great.) We used Pick-a-time and actually used it again during our school closure #Covid19 graduation for families to pick their time for their individual ceremonies. Ensure you are signed up and connected electronically to the app, website, email blasts, etc.

104. WRITING EMAILS TO YOUR KIDS' TEACHERS

It can be hard to read or feel the tone in an email. They also never go away, so be mindful when writing emails to your kid's teacher. Again, there are usually three sides to every story—your kid's side, the teacher's side, and then the action that actually occurred in the exact way it occurred. So, when writing to your kids' teachers, keep it short, keep it simple, and be clear. If your kid is complaining about something that happened during school, don't write a long accusatory email. Email the teacher and either ask for a phone call or email in return providing some clarity on the situation. Here's an example: Your kid comes home and says Johnny was pushing him in the schoolyard and that he told the teacher and the teacher did nothing. Do not write an email asking why they did not do anything when your son was being pushed and assaulted. Rather phrase it more like this: "Dear Mr. Teacher: Can you please provide some clarity on the situation that may have occurred yesterday during recess? My child told me he informed you that Johnny was pushing him, and he spoke to you about it. Can you please let me know if indeed that occurred and anything else? I am available from such-and-such a time if you would like to call, and/or I will await your response via email. Thank you in advance. Kind regards, Mr. Marotta."

So many times, parents jump to conclusions because they are emotional and upset about whatever it is their child is telling them. Take a deep breath, and things do not always appear as they seem (see tip #54 FEAR). Many students tell their parents something totally false and/or that did not happen in the way they told it, so do your best to seek clarity in the situation. If you are very upset, my recommendation is to write the email, yet DO NOT HIT SEND. Re-read it in the morning, edit, and maybe have a trusted second set of eyes look at it, then send. Work with your child's teachers, not against them.

105. IF YOU DO NOT KNOW WHAT TO SAY, DON'T SAY ANYTHING.

This is one that I take from my world of officiating college basketball. I hung up the stripes at the end of the 2019 season to invest more time with my family. I fell in love with a passion different from officiating: the world of writing and professional development for school leaders. This tip has helped me in many situations. This hasn't come easily, and I worked hard to embed it in the forefront of my brain. Teach your child that when they don't know what to say, don't say anything. It's kind of like the old saying when we were kids: If you don't have anything nice to say, don't say anything at all.

So much drama in schools is because kids either say something, or now, in today's world, they write things on social media. Zip it. I never saw a discipline referral at school where a child was in a situation, whether it was with a teacher or another student, that read Johnny was being corrected by a staff member, and Johnny looked him in the eye, nodded, and did not say anything. That just doesn't happen. Teach your kids to know when to keep their mouths closed, especially if they don't know what to say—not as extreme as with law-enforcement, where someone may be read their Miranda rights. Yet it is in the same ballpark: if you don't know what to say, don't say anything.

106. SEEK TO UNDERSTAND BEFORE BEING UNDERSTOOD.

Love this. I learned this from the great *7 Habits of Highly Effective People* book and training. Also, from my wonderful wife. I am a talk first, act first, move quick type leader, which I know isn't always the best. I have tried and have gotten better to slow down, not react so fast, and not strike first. Think about this and the concept of "seek to understand before being understood."

Simply put, this concept asks you to pause your interest, listen, take a deeper look, and try to absorb all BEFORE you dive in. So many times, schools push out information to the masses, and maybe it wasn't clear. Maybe there wasn't enough, yet try to understand first. I remember a parent, Genny Cornell, who wrote a beautiful excerpt earlier in the book (tip #81), reached out to me after freshmen orientation that I ran at our HS. It was her first child coming through the school. She was nervous, yet looking to absorb all the information and prepare her son, Sean. She read the letters, looked on the website, and came to our orientation. A few days later, she asked to meet with me, and so I did. She was great—didn't attack me or insult, yet just respectfully said, "This wasn't enough." I need more to understand what is going to happen.

For me, she did her best to understand first and was correct in her assessment; we weren't doing enough to provide clarity for our parents and students. Then, respectfully and in the best way ever, she gave me excellent feedback and actually became part of the solution, also being a guest speaker multiple times to incoming parents and freshmen. She helped me understand what was needed.

TECHNOLOGY & SOCIAL MEDIA

" *You are responsible for everything you post on social media and everything you post will be a reflection of you.*"

— *GERMANY KENT, JOURNALIST, SOCIAL MEDIA ETIQUETTE EXPERT*

I t is our role as parents to guide and lead our children in all they do. We are technology and social media transplants; the children are natives. They've grown up with it. These are decisions you will have to make when and how you will allow and introduce social media and technology use for your children. Just like many issues they will face growing up, you can't block them forever, yet you have to teach them to be responsible and upstanding in their representations of themselves and your family. There are several examples and stories of this topic in Chapter Nine.

107. SOCIAL MEDIA

Like many concepts in this book, each family is different, each child is different, and each teaching point impacts families differently. My advice when discussing social media with parents is to start slowly and manage your child along the way. Remember, we as parents are immigrants to social media, whereas our children are natives. They're growing up with these sites and apps, and we did not. Slow and steady. As I write this book, our oldest child is in eighth grade. She got her first cell phone in sixth grade. She did not have any social media when she began and has watched many of her classmates have issues and problems on social media like Snapchat and TikTok. In addition to going slow and steady with your child and their phones and social media accounts, create some clear ground rules that are non-negotiable:

1. Mom and dad have access to your accounts. (Be mindful if sometimes they create second ones that you are not aware of.)
2. No inappropriate, unclothed photos of yourself. Ever. Under any circumstances. Simply put, do not put photos on there that you would not want to share with your grandma.
3. Before posting, ask yourself, "is it positive, is it necessary, is it helpful, is it thoughtful, is it true?"

Many issues with teens and adults happen because their posts are negative in nature or critical of others. Teach your child like the ways of the Jedi in Star Wars: use your power for good, not evil. Use your social media sites to help others or lift others' spirits up and not drag them down. Additionally, so many colleges and employers now look at social media sites as an informal way of making decisions about their acceptance into school or should they hire the person or not. Think back into recent news: a professional athlete, a political figure, a local educator has something negative come out about their social media that they posted many, many years ago? It sure does happen. Start slowly with your children and teach them along the way, and have the mindset that you and your child want your social media sites to be something that will help them down the road and not hurt them.

Sadly, I have seen several young people arrested, charged, denied college, denied the military and job opportunities because of things they have put on social media, things they have liked, and people they follow. Most importantly, have a conversation with your child about photos and sexting. These can be the most damaging. A young lady who is head over heels in love with her boyfriend takes a nude photo of herself and shares it with him with the promise that he would never share it with anyone else. We've all heard the stories, and I have first-hand seen the results and the damage it does to a young lady whose photo spread through the school like wildfire. It is upsetting and an all-powerful negative impact on that young lady and her family. The sense of helplessness and regret overwhelm them while school administrators and staff scramble to stop the damage.

This can also become troublesome for the young men or women who possess and/or forward this type of material. There are ever-changing laws and rules about this so please, urge your children to be mindful and respectful.

We educate our students about the power of not forwarding inappropriate texts, photos, and social media posts and empower them to "see something, say something." This is a most sensitive topic, and I strongly encourage you to be open and honest with your children, walking alongside them, and staying close during their journey as pre-teens, teenagers, and young adults.

108. CELL PHONE: BABY STEPS

When it comes time for the cell phone, take baby steps. There is so much to it, and certainly, the hope is they use it for good, yet I caution you to take it slow. If you train your child early about the rules and your expectations with the phone, you hopefully will be raising a digitally respectful young citizen. It cannot be like Legos: Just give it to them and let them go, be creative, go searching, and go off on your own. With Legos or similar toys, you want them exploring and doing it on their own. Cell phone: my opinion, no-no! Open up doors and more freedom as you go. Giving an 11-, 12-, 13-, or 14-year-old a phone with no restrictions is a recipe for disaster. Take, for example, apps. You can put a restriction that the child has to ask to get a certain app before they just download it. There is so much out there on the internet and beyond that can all come way too fast to your kid if you do not slow it down. Take it slow; let them earn more trust as they grow older and more responsible. As my dad told me when I was a kid, "I don't care what so and so's family is doing. That is not for our family or for you!" I heard this 100 + times in my life. You get your kid a cell phone when you are ready and when they are ready, not anyone else!

109. BE MINDFUL OF TECHNOLOGY IN THEIR ROOM.

Like many things, start slow, and start more restrictive than not. I wrote earlier, like we all heard as kids, that nothing good happens after midnight; well, here is a similar comparison: nothing good will happen if a young pre-teen or teen is in their room with their phone or computer with the door closed. We are thrilled that we started this early with our kids. Phones stay downstairs and are charged downstairs. Do a short experiment: keep your kids phone with you with 2-

TECHNOLOGY & SOCIAL MEDIA

hour blocks at different times, including keeping it overnight. See how many notifications they get in those times, especially the night-time. Think about how many times they would be disrupted from their sleep with those notifications? Is it worth it? Phones downstairs with restrictions until they get a little older. If they are older and out of control with the phone? Take it, just like that. Do you pay the bill? Did you buy it? Then if they are not doing the right things, take it away until they learn.

Additionally, it is not all bad. My daughter Claire is actually very helpful with the phones: helping us with some tech issues, setting it up for her grandparents, and now as she grows, helpful sharing apps, including her bank account. So, as the Jedi shared in Star Wars, train your children to use their phones for good, not evil, between the hours of 9am-9pm!

110. DON'T GET ALL YOUR INFORMATION FROM FACEBOOK.

I'm new to Facebook. And I really only use it professionally to share information and share our educational concepts and such. I certainly do enjoy seeing family photos and reading family news as people update their lives. I caution you, though, to not use it as an information source for ongoings at school. Facebook is people's opinion, and it can become the modern game of Telephone. If something is going on at school, especially a crisis or an emergency situation, be mindful of the information that is on Facebook. People can get very emotional and can get going negatively, especially the comments. There can be a lot of valuable information shared through Facebook, but I caution you regarding facts versus people's opinions or experience. Get your information from a valid source. Certainly, if it comes directly from the school's Facebook page, I can understand, yet be mindful of people's comments along the way.

111. "I'M NOT GOOD AT COMPUTERS."

As I completed this book, we were in the throes of the #coronavirus pandemic. This is a tough time for so many worldwide, and my heart goes out to those who experienced tremendous loss. One group that was definitely at a disadvantage was parents who are not up to date on using technology. For years, I heard those older than me say things like, "I'm not good at computers," or "I don't know how to use a smartphone." I believe this is part of our duty as parents to maybe not necessarily be an expert at these devices and new technologies, yet at least be aware of how it works. I think it is important to model a growth mindset for our children in all areas. The kids are probably better at using most of the technology, so even better, have them teach you. That comment, "I'm not good at computers," has always rubbed me the wrong way. It's an excuse, not a fact. Learn and give it a try. You will demonstrate that when things are not easy or new for you, that you can do anything if you put your mind to it. Learn technology no matter what your age.

112. DON'T SETTLE SCORES ON SOCIAL MEDIA.

People are going to upset your children. People will offend your children. Bad things will happen to your children. Teach them not to settle scores on social media. How did we do this when we were kids? We worked it out. We spoke to the person. We stayed away from the person, maybe made some different decisions, etc. Maybe even beat them out for that spot on the team or beat them in that competitive game of dodgeball. Time healed those wounds, and we moved on as life moved on. Social media words, pictures, and posts extend these hurt feelings and even deepen them.

Your children do not have to voice every feeling they have on social media, especially when it is one of anger or frustration. We have to continue to model and teach our children healthy ways to release their frustrations and express their feelings. Being critical or vengeful of others while everyone can read these feelings is not a good situation. Nothing good will come of it, so teach and model for your child another more purposeful and productive way.

PARENTING & COACHING

> *Your kid's success or lack of success in sports does not indicate what kind of parent you are. Having an athlete that is coachable, respectful, a great teammate, mentally tough, resilient, and who tries their best is a direct reflection of your parenting.*

> — *AUTHOR UNKNOWN*

The points in this chapter will help you and your child on and off the fields and courts. Years after the games have passed, it should not be about the scores or minutes played, yet about their experience, relationships with teammates and coaches, and enjoying the journey.

113. I CAN DO THIS.

Your child will have many pressure-filled experiences along their educational journey. Whether it is the first day of kindergarten, that first-day picking seats in the cafeteria, tryouts, dating, driving, etc. So many firsts and so many challenges along the way. A simple thing I picked up from my mentor, Dr. Robert Gilbert, are these four simple words: I can do this. It's so simple, yet self-talk is so important. Try this. Put your thumb to your pointer finger and start with the letter "I." Next, move your thumb to your middle finger and say the word "can." Next, your ring finger, and say the word "do," and then end with your thumb on your pinky finger and say "this." Teach your kid this mental exercise early and often. "I can do this," and move your thumb over the four fingertips. Over and over.

This simple mental exercise will strengthen your child's confidence, simplify an event, and create a strong belief in themselves. Try it yourself. You hearing yourself out loud and in your head telling yourself that YOU CAN DO IT is really important. So many times, demons and self-doubting creep into our minds and hearts, affecting our confidence. This simple action can help block out these negative thoughts. There are moments even we, as parents, still have challenges that we are trying to get through, and this simple exercise can help. It certainly can become a very important confidence builder for your child.

114. E+R=O EVENT PLUS RESPONSE = OUTCOME.

Which letter do you think is the most important in this equation? Many would say "O" outcome. We want to have great outcomes in our lives and also for our children. Who doesn't? Yet R is the most important. There will be many events, opportunities, and challenges for your children throughout their journey, and some will work out, and some won't. Yet, it is the response that determines the outcome for your children. Throughout this book, I share things you can do along the way to help those outcomes, but how your child responds to all of the events that happened throughout their journey is key. Continue to remind them and reinforce the message of, "things will happen." Circumstances will not work out. Opportunities will come and go, yet we must continue to respond positively, make good choices, and continue to script the outcomes we want by creating great responses to the things in and around our children's lives.

115. LOOKING FOR AN OKG

I had the great privilege of interviewing my college basketball coach, John Thompson, years later on my podcast *#ELB: Education Leadership and Beyond*. Coach T, as we fondly called him, spent several years at Guilford as the assistant during my time there, then went on to be the head coach and athletic director for many years at North Carolina Wesleyan College. Doing the interview, I asked coach Thompson what types of players does he look for while recruiting new student-athletes. He very simply stated, "We are looking for "OKG,." was his response. OKGs? Yes, OKGs: *Our kinda gals/guys.* He explained what OKGs are and what they stand for: student-athletes that arrive early, are selfless, have a positive attitude, looking to contribute to something greater than themselves, a great teammate, are all in, etc. Having great athletic talent is certainly something they look for, but the character and makeup of the person are much more important. That's the definition of an OKG, and he is looking to fill not only his roster but his school with these types of student-athletes.

I think it is a great concept, and I have adopted it in my hiring practices as a school leader. Be an #OKG.

116. ENERGY & ENTHUSIASM: THE STORY OF FRANK BETTGER

As an exercise, my friend Dr. Rob Gilbert challenged me to read the first chapter of the book *How I Raised Myself from Failure to Success in Selling, 1977* by Frank Bettger. And not just read it, but read it every day for 30 days in a row. Whoa, yet I did it, and it worked. It inspired me to be more enthusiastic in all I did.

The story is Frank was a budding minor leaguer in baseball in the early 1900s. The manager called him and said he was shipping him out of town. Frank, shocked, asked why and was told he was lazy. Frank explained that he wasn't being lazy, but was just trying to take it easy to downplay his nervousness. The manager said it will never work and fired him. Frank wound up in one of the lowest leagues there was near Philadelphia. When he arrived, he promised himself he would never be told he was lazy again and decided he would play like he was on fire. He wanted to establish a new reputation for being the most enthusiastic ballplayer in the league. Bettger (1986) writes in Chapter One, " From the minute I appeared on the field, I acted like a man electrified. I acted as though I were alive with a million batteries. I threw the ball around the diamond so fast and so hard that it almost knocked the infielders' hands apart....

"Did it work? It worked like magic. Three things happened.

1. "My enthusiasm almost entirely overcame my fear and nervousness..."
2. "My enthusiasm affected the other players on the team, and they too became enthusiastic."

3. "Instead of tiring during the game, I felt better during the game, and after it was over than I had ever felt before."

Bettger shares that he took the same approach when his playing days ended due to an injury when he turned to sales. He became the most enthusiastic speaker and salesperson, and he made millions in sales. It truly is a great story, and I hope to tell it one day in a #TED talk. I encourage you to order and read the first chapter with your child. It just may rub on both of you. It certainly has for me.

117. HOW TO PARENT AN ATHLETE DURING A GLOBAL PANDEMIC BY DR. DEANA STEVENSON

Dr. Deana Stevenson is the founder of DocDeanaEnterprises. She leads and coaches school administrators from around the country, guiding them in leading their schools. She is also a medical doctor and married to Dr. Bert Stevenson, a school administrator from Orchard Park, NY. Follow her on Instagram at @docdeanaen-terprises.

We've all heard that children don't come with directions, so even if there were a playbook on parenting, none of us would have the chapter related to a Global Pandemic.

There were so many tough decisions to make and, in some instances, in a matter of days. Should my child use the hybrid method of instruction or go fully remote? Will we allow our children to take the school bus or be responsible for getting them to and from school for the entire school year?

All of these decisions were tough, and they required weighing the pros and cons of each choice. Now add that these decisions were being made for our daughter, a 6'4" high school junior. Whatever decision we made would ultimately impact her future as a college basketball player.

Before March 13, 2020, our daughter was heavily recruited by some of the top basketball programs in the country. Preparations and plans were in place to visit schools throughout the summer, in addition to playing in Amateur Athletic Union (AAU) tournaments from NYC to LA. So when the world as we know it shuts down, what happens to recruitment? It stops!

How does one parent an athlete during a Global Pandemic? Parents become recruitment agents. In a Global Pandemic, recruitment and college visits become multiple daily telephone calls and virtual campus visits. Multiple AAU basketball tournaments turn into "pick-up games" and intense workouts, both of which are videotaped and sent to coaches by parents.

Parenting involves reassuring your daughter that this season of uncertainty will build character, resilience, and amazing relationships with coaches. Parenting an athlete means being laser-focused, optimistic, and viewing the obstacles not as barriers to your child's future, but as benchmarks to build your child's character.

So, how do you parent an athlete during a global pandemic? The same way you would parent if we were not going through a global pandemic... With love. You parent knowing that there's more to life than the sport. You take advantage of the extra time you have by planning family meals where everyone assists. You take longer walks with your child because you are not rushed to get to the next practice. You listen more attentively because your child athlete is home and not at the gym. You binge-watch their favorite show on a paid on-demand streaming service and live within the moment.

Most importantly, you make a commitment to your child athlete that when the Global Pandemic ends (and it will) that these stolen moments of connecting with them outside of their sport continue. You commit to not making life all about their sport and the next practice. You recommit yourself to them as their parent and realize they are more than the sport they play. They are more than the tournaments and college visits. Parenting an athlete during a Global Pandemic has been the best experience for us because it has caused us to recommit our priorities. Yes, being an athlete is important to our daughter and our family. However, being a parent and enjoying the process is far more important.

118. I'M NOT EVEN ON THE LIST.

July 2006, Indianapolis, Indiana. I am trying out to become a member of the Atlantic Coast Conference (ACC) and Colonial officiating staff. I have one year of Division 1 experience refereeing in The Patriot and Ivy League's men's basketball league, as well as five years of college experience overall. When I arrived at the hotel, I met the young lady registering the officials and checking them in. She handed me a roster of the people who were there trying out. There were 25 names on the list. When I said to her I don't see my name, she said, *oh don't worry, we have your name; it's just not on that list.* I answered, "how come?" She replied that *somebody was not able to make it, so we filled you in their slot.* I stepped away from the registration area and quickly realized I was a B invite. I was not even in their first selections to the camp, yet was just a fill-in for someone who could not make it. This made me angry inside and even more determined to do a good job. From my inner gut came the mindset of, "I'll show them." I did not want to waste my time or money to be there, so I decided to give it everything I had.

Midway through the tryout, the supervisor, John Clougherty, who wound up becoming a good friend and mentor to me, walked on the court and whispered in my ear during the game. "I don't know who you are or where you are from, but I like you, and I'm going to hire you. Keep your mouth shut and do a good job." With that, he patted me on the back, and I continued on.

I share this story because there will be similar experiences along the way for your children. Whether it's being left off the roster for the school play, not making the team, or just not being in the perfect circumstance for some activity they are involved in. If I had shut down at that moment and let my frustrations get the best of me, how would I have performed? Would I have gone out there determined and focused or frustrated and angry? Would my body language have given the wrong message? That experience restored my faith in a lot of things, including a great attitude and hard work that can put you in great spots and opportunities. I went on to referee in those leagues and more for 20 years and had a great experience. Things might have been different for me if I just concluded at that moment that this was going to be a waste of my time—#makethebestofyourcircumstances.

119. 1390 & 199

Pretty random numbers. Nothing to them, except that they are Mike Piazza's and Tom Brady's draft numbers. Yes, the number they were selected in their respective draft years, 1988 and 2000. Most know how their stories turned out but, if you don't, here is a brief summary: Mike Piazza went on to a Hall of Fame career with the Dodgers and Mets. Piazza played 16 years and hit 427 career home runs, including a major league record 396 as a catcher. A 12-time All-Star, Piazza won 10 Silver Slugger Awards and finished in the top five in MVP voting four times. In short, he had an amazing career.

Brady, at the time of publication, just joined the Tampa Bay Buccaneers. He is a six-time Super Bowl champ and arguably one of the best quarterbacks to ever play the game.

The moral of the stories and of the numbers are many. Simply put, it's not where you start; it's where you finish. Also, don't let others' opinions of your kids' athletic talent (or any talent) be the end all be all. It is not the number of times you fail that counts; it is the number of times you keep trying and succeed that really counts. If they don't make the team, keep trying. If they don't get the starting job, keep trying. If they get injured, keep trying. There is no way you can fail/they can fail if you teach your child to keep working, keep trying, keep up the right attitude, and #keeprolling.

Tom Brady ✓
@TomBrady

I got a chance to hold my draft card a few hours ago.
Never forget where you came from.

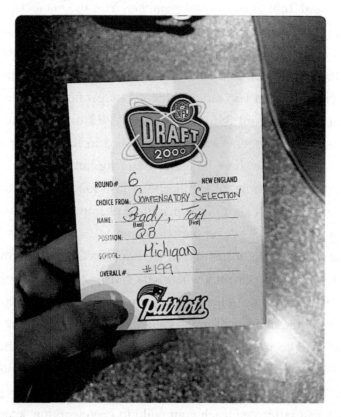

120. YOU CAN WEAR MINE.

The year is 2019, and Port Jervis (NY) football is having an amazing season. After a few challenging seasons, our coach stepped down, and we hired a new coach. It was a remarkable season. There were many highs and memorable moments. This one story did not make the headlines or the stat sheet, yet it won my heart instantly, and I am grateful to this young man for his sacrifice.

Playoff time: Port had a big game on the road. The kids, coaches, and community were buzzing with excitement. We traveled over an hour and a half to arrive at the game site. The locker rooms were filled with activity, music, testosterone, and a star receiver panicking, looking for his cleats. He realized he left them home. With his family already in the stands, there was not much he could do. Then Sam (I changed this young man's name, yet really want him to have the recognition) came over to the star player and said, "You can wear mine." They happened to be the same size. Sam was a senior who had never been on the team before and rarely played. At this moment, Sam put the betterment of the team above the embarrassment of him being on the sideline in sneakers, and in a selfless act, helped out his team. Even writing this, I get goosebumps for what this young man did at that moment. As a great story would have it, the star player had an amazing game catching two touchdowns and making several game-changing plays.

What Sam did was just awesome. He put it all above his pride and preparedness to serve others. While every kid can't be a star, let's teach our kids this lesson, to give of ourselves to others. Dr. Gilbert shares on his hotline: "Don't try to be the best on the team, be the best for the team." Way to go, Sam!

121. IF AT A YOUTH SPORTING EVENT, IF YOUR WORDS START WITH A VERB, YOU ARE NOT CHEERING; YOU ARE COACHING!

Throw it! Shoot it! Pass and so on and so on. Don't coach your children during games. Coach them, guide them, teach them, encourage them all the other time, yet not during the game. Leave them be and let the coaches coach them during the games. Enjoy the games. Cheer. Encourage. Wave the towel and be a fan: just don't coach your kid, and certainly do not make comments about other kids.

I have really tried to not have many *don'ts* in this book, to keep things positive, and encouraged many *do*s. Yet this one is pretty straightforward: Don't coach your kids during games.

As we all know, fan behavior at school sporting events can be quite poor at times. We had some parent issues over my time as Principal: berating referees, parents yelling at other kids on the team, parents getting into it with other fans from other schools, parents coaching their kid against the coach's instructions, etc. Just be mindful: you are not at a pro football game that you can yell whatever you want. There are kids and families nearby. Have fun, enjoy your kid out on the field or court. I remember my dad at my games as a kid sitting way up at the top of the stands at several events, away from the pack of fans from my team, who were all in a group. I asked, "Dad, why are you way up there away from everyone? And you are not even cheering me on?" He responded that I would understand one day and that he was cheering me on, just not yelling out loud. In summary, don't coach your kid from the stands at games. Let them be and enjoy the moment.

122. REDSHIRTING

I love the author Malcolm Gladwell. I think he is brilliant, a great storyteller, and provides excellent content for various people and, in this case, parents. In his book, *Outliers*, he tells the story of the hockey all-stars in Canada. The cut-off date for hockey sign-ups in Canada is December 31. After a thorough study of 10+ years, Gladwell writes that most of the all-stars in the Canadian youth hockey leagues were born in January, February, and March. Why was this the case? In looking at it more deeply, Gladwell writes that these children had a physical advantage over the others because of when they were born. A child born in January who is competing against a child born in October is 10 months older than that child. As adults, that's not a big difference, but as children who are growing and developing, this is a huge advantage. They have 10 more months of further motor skills and muscular development than the others, leading to superior athletic skills. With these superior skills, these children will play more during the season, experience success more often, and make all-star teams. Once all-star, several things happen: this is a boost in their confidence, they are exposed to better players, they get more ice time, they are exposed to the best coaches, etc., etc. All of these are points that lead to success for that child. So what does this have to do with education?

Gladwell goes on to describe that it is quite similar in schools. The student that is born closer to the cut-off date in a particular school district has an advantage over the child who is near the end of that cut-off. Let's compare the hockey players to reading levels. The student who is close to the cut-off has a 10- or 11- month advantage over the child near the end of the calendar, and think about that in terms of a second or third grader who is learning how to read. Ten months further of brain development in that child could lead to an advantage over another much younger student. So their brain is more developed, they have an opportunity to become a stronger reader, achieve higher on exams, state tests, and reading activities, which produce similar results as the child who makes the All-Star team—a boost in confidence, opportunities for gifted and honors programs, etc. It is a fascinating and thought-provoking situation for parents to consider for their children.

In our own personal decision for our family, my wife and I weighed many factors. I met with superintendents, principals, elementary teachers, and others and asked the question, "Should we wait to enroll our child when they are five years old in kindergarten or six?"

The overwhelming answer that my wife and I received was if we financially could afford it, and/or our family set up was such that we could wait, that we should. This would allow us to have our child stay home one more year with us in those most precious years. Additionally, they encouraged us if we were going to wait to have them start school until they were six, that we should find enrichment activities and things to engage them academically until that starting point. This was a wise piece of information and an important component of their development. My wife and I wound up "redshirting" both our two older children, Claire and Matthew, and have had great results in school and their development. Our third Tessa is a different story and was a different fit. My wife returned to work and actually got a job in the elementary school that the children attended.

Additionally, Tessa watched her two older siblings for the first five years of her life read books, do their homework, and be engaged in school. She did plenty of that herself, too, so when she was five, we felt that she was more than ready. She was chomping at the bit to start school and has never looked back since. So the decision for each family will be different because each circumstance and each child is different, so you will make the best choices for yourself and your family. In the end, you will make the right decision.

123. JOE MCCARTHY'S 10 COMMANDMENTS OF BASEBALL (1949)

I love these. They cross over into so many parts of our lives and offer such great lessons that go way beyond the baseball field. Coach McCarthy managed the Cubs, Yankees, and the Red Sox for almost 25 years in the majors.

1. Nobody ever became a ballplayer by walking after a ball.

2. You will never become a .300 hitter unless you take the bat off your shoulder.

3. An outfielder who throws in back of a runner is locking the barn after the horse is stolen.

4. Keep your head up, and you may not have to keep it down.

5. When you start to slide, slide. He who changes his mind may have to change a good leg for a bad one.

6. Do not alibi on bad hops. Anybody can field the good ones.

7. Always run them out. You never can tell.

8. Do not quit.

9. Do not fight too much with umpires. You cannot expect them to be as perfect as you are.

10. A pitcher who hasn't control hasn't anything.

124. PODCASTS

How do you sharpen your saw as a parent? What type of training or professional development do you do to become a better parent? Hopefully, reading this book can help you, but there are a ton of resources out there. Whether it is parenting classes, self-improvement classes, couples weekend getaways, or even books and podcasts. One of the ones that has helped me as a father is " The Dad Edge" by Larry Hagner. Larry has written many books and has a weekly podcast on which he has various guests. I have listened for several years and really have responded to Larry's words and his guests. I have grown spiritually, taken financial advice, and opened up about patience, as well as intimacy and privacy, within marriage. These are all tremendous topics that can make or break a marriage, and what do they say is the best thing parents can do for their children? Love each other!

Invest your time in sharpening the saw to improve yourself as a parent, spouse, and person. There are so many varieties and methods out there, so choose the one for you. My friend Larry Hagner and "The Dad Edge" is just one of many examples out there, but one that has really worked for me.

125. BE WHERE YOU ARE SUPPOSED TO BE AND DO WHAT YOU ARE SUPPOSED TO DO.

Coach Gelston was the 1967-1991 Men's Basketball Head Coach at Montclair State University in New Jersey. How very simple this tip #125. This could not be spelled out any more clearly. *Be where you are supposed to be and do what you are supposed to do.* I think about all of the problems that this would solve in situations that your child would stay out of because of these two simple rules. Say this repeatedly to your child, and only good things can come of it. This is from the long-time basketball coach at Montclair State University, who is a legend at that college. My friend Dr. Rob Gilbert gave me a plaque that hangs in my office today. Keep it simple, be where you are supposed to be, and do what you are supposed to do. That encompasses a lot and may keep your kid out of jams in the future.

One very delicate conversation that you are going to have with your child is about recreational drugs. As I write this book, I'm 45-years-old and have never smoked or tried marijuana. It was just something that I was never really around, exposed to, and knew that it wasn't something I should get involved with. My parents spoke to me often about drugs and, as I grew into my teen years, it never became an issue. I guess in listening to this quote by Coach Gill, my staying away from drugs can fall into this category: Be where you were supposed to be and do what you were supposed to do. If you are never at parties, places, or around people who are using drugs, chances are that your child won't, so embed this in their routines and echo it in their ears.

126. YOU ARE A PARENT AND A COACH FOR YOUR CHILD—LESSONS FROM ONE OF THE GREATEST: JOHN WOODEN.

Steve Broadwell, an educator, school leader, and coach from upstate New York in the North Country, used to write many coaches back when he was a coach and athletic director. One of them was the great John Wooden. Unbelievably, when Steve wrote to Coach Wooden asking about things that he could do with his team to be successful, this is what Coach Wooden wrote back. Yes, Steve Broadwell received a handwritten letter from The Wizard himself. This advice is priceless, goes way beyond just sports, and I thank Steve for allowing me to share it in the book. All the points are incredibly purposeful and brilliant, but pay particular attention to the last one, number 14. Really, is there anything else?

1. Be quick but not in a hurry.
2. Stay in balance—physically, mentally, and emotionally.
3. Do not try to be better than someone else, but never cease trying to be the best you can be.
4. More championships are won by being strong defensively than by being strong offensively
5. I would prefer that most of our field goals come after a pass rather than at the end of a dribble.
6. Assume every shot will be missed and move quickly to your rebounding area.
7. Be more interested in your character than your reputation.

8. My responsibility for your physical condition will take place during our practice periods. Your responsibility comes from your ACTIONS from between practices.

9. I see no reason for excessive jubilation for out-scoring an opponent in a game nor reason for excessive dejection when you are outscored.

10. Failure to prepare is preparing to fail.

11. Get ready, and then, perhaps your chance will come.

12. Fill your role to the very best of your ability.

13. Never permit yourself to get concerned regarding things over which you have no control

14. Earn the right to respect by being: Industrious, friendly, loyal, cooperative, courteous, enthusiastic, self-disciplined, clean, neat, and considerate of others.

From the desk of...

JOHN WOODEN

10-10-89

Dear Coach Broadwell,

Here are a few ideas that I tried to get across to my UCLA players each and every year.

1. Be quick, but do not hurry.

2. Stay in balance — physically, mentally, and emotionally

3. Do not try to be better than someone else, but never cease trying to be the best that you can be.

4. More championships are won by being strong defensively than being strong offensively.

5. I would prefer that most of our field goals come after a pass rather than at the end of a dribble.

6. Assume every shot will be missed and move quickly to your rebounding area.

From the desk of...

JOHN WOODEN

7. Be more interested in your character than your reputation.

8. My responsibility for your physical condition will take place during our practice periods, your responsibility comes from your actions between practices.

9. I see no reason for excessive jubilation for outscoring an opponent in a game, nor reason for excessive dejection when you are outscored.

10. Failure to prepare is preparing to fail.

11. Get ready and then, perhaps, your chance will come.

12. Fill your role to the very best of your ability.

13. Never permit yourself to get too concerned in regard to things over which you have no control.

From the desk of...

JOHN WOODEN

14. Earn the right to respect by being —

Industrious, Friendly, Loyal, Cooperative, Courteous, Enthusiastic, Self-disciplined, Clean, Neat, and considerate of others.

Best wishes for a very successful season.

Sincerely,

John Wooden

127. EVERYONE LIKES TO WIN ON SATURDAY.

The great Bobby Knight (although his sideline behavior is a different argument), former college basketball coach, used to say that everyone likes to win on Saturdays. Yet, not everyone wants to practice hard on Tuesdays. The fans in the stands, eyes watching on TV, and all those watching see the victorious players and think it was easy because the great ones make it look easy. What people don't see is the work the superior athletes put in: the behind-the-scenes each and every day— the hours of practice, the repetition, the training. Sometimes, kids can think it comes easy because it looks easy. The real concept is that your kid can become great at anything if they work at it, and I am not just talking about sports. Think of the 5000-hour rule. Do something for 5000 hours, and you are going to become an expert. So remind your child as they are going through the sporting ranks or even academic pursuits at school that it takes a while. Have that stick-with-it attitude and put the time in.

128. GO TO THE GAMES.

I know you are busy. I know you have pressures. I know your mind might be somewhere else. Even as I write this book, I am away from my kids right now. I get it, but I am not missing one of their games.

I am writing this point to urge you to attend your child's games. I share that powerful story in the first point in the book about my dad coming down to Virginia from NY on a weeknight. Here I am twenty-five years later writing about it. It meant so much to me and left such an impact on him and my mom's care and love for me. Now, hopefully, you will not have to travel eight-plus hours to each game, but go to the games. It goes quick, and I am not talking about the games themselves. I am talking about the time...the time when your child will be playing.

Let's do some quick math. Let's say your kid makes the modified or middle school team in seventh grade. If they make junior varsity and varsity in HS, that will be a total of six years of playing sports. If they have fifteen games a year, how many games will they have? That's right, ninety—ninety games over six years. Now let's shave a few off: sick, weather, injury and work obligations may be where you can't make the game. I'll be generous and say twenty. Twenty games that you/your child/cancellations will impact or cause you to miss the game. Now we are down to seventy games in six years. They are precious. It is such a small window so make it a priority and be there. Get your lawn chair, your seat cushion, your koozie, your vizor, and whatever else you need to be there...and be there. Maybe your kid will be writing about you in twenty-five years!

129. GLAD YOU DID OR WISH YOU WOULD HAVE?

Well, that's about it—just one more tip for you. I hope you enjoyed these stories and anecdotes. It is my hope that your relationship with your child, their journey through school, your family's experiences with the school will all work out for the best. I hope these tips helped...and that they made you think, reflect, and take action.

I have heard many times that it is the things that we didn't do that we regret the most. When we look back, what will we think, say? What will the kids think, say? I believe that if you act on most of these tips (I can't expect that you will love each one), you will create rich, authentic, meaningful experiences for your child through their K-12 journey. You will empower your child. You will build lasting, positive relationships with school staff. You can also look back and be proud of the work you put in for the success of your child, so digest that question before you throw this book down: Are you glad you did or wish you would have? Put it into action!

GRATITUDE MINDSET

 Gratitude: It's the mother of all virtues."

— DR. STEPHEN BIRCHAK, PSYCHOLOGIST AND

PROFESSOR

130. GRATITUDE

I am 13-years-old, and my Dad is driving me to a pool party at a friend's house. I grew up in Staten Island, NY, and this particular party was at someone's house who lived on Todt Hill, a very wealthy area of Staten Island. At the time, my parents were driving an old clunker, a brown Plymouth from the 70s that had a huge dent in the side (see Chapter 4 Truths: They will lie).

This is the actual plate from the car. I keep it in my office to help me remember to be grateful for the people, things, and opportunities I have in my life.

I was really excited about the party, and even put a little extra gel in my hair! As we were approaching the house, I felt a wave of embarrassment overwhelm me. I began to sweat because I was so embarrassed by how junky the car was. (This was the car from tip #57, the Plymouth Fury) I blurted out, "Dad, you don't have to drive me all the way. I don't want you to have to drive anymore."

He said, "No, no. I'll drive you. Not a problem. I already drove you this far." We went back and forth like this a few times until he realized the reason for my plea. If you grew up in the '60s or '70s, you'd know exactly what I am talking about with this. He pulled over and threw the car in park. The gear shift was on the column of the steering wheel, so with his right hand, he forcefully pushed the car into park (probably why the transmission was always busted!), jerking the car to a halt. He whipped around enraged, grabbed me by the collar, pulled me in close to him, almost nose-to-nose. I could feel the heat from his breath.

Clenching his teeth, he said, "Don't you ever be embarrassed by what we have! This is the car that we can afford. Be grateful for what we have. Be grateful for your family!" With that, he drove the remaining two blocks in silence to the house. "Enjoy the party," he said as I shamefully exited the car. I was so ashamed that I acted in this way and disappointed my dad. It was hard for me to understand at that moment, yet here I am, 32 years later, writing about it. It was so profound, and really what it is all about is being grateful—grateful for your life, your family, your career, your education, your children, their talents...I could go on and on.

I write this final chapter in the days of the Coronavirus in December 2020. I look and listen to all that is happening around us, people scraping and clawing to make ends meet, people who are sick, who passed away, who've been furloughed, and more. I am grateful. Grateful to be home with my family. To have food to provide, charades to play, and time together, and the ability to write. My mind races with ideas and thoughts, sometimes feeling like a Nascar race in my head, like the words of Hamilton, "Write like I am running out of time!"

No matter the circumstance you will face as a parent, whether you are just starting out, or are a seasoned veteran, lead with gratitude. Have a gratitude mindset. My friend Dr. Stephen Birchak, psychology Professor and St. Thomas Aquinas College in NY, said to our school district during his workshop: "Gratitude: It is the greatest and mother of all the virtues. If you lead with gratitude, everything else follows."

It is my hope that this book inspired you and challenged your thinking. I guess you read it because you want your child to do well in school, and you want to support them as best you can. Maybe not: maybe you got it as a re-gift at a secret Santa party. Maybe it was the last gift at a 50-50 PTA raffle? Maybe you just stumbled upon a bookstore and were curious. Whatever the reason, you got to the end, and I hope you enjoyed it. Put some or all of these into action. When you look back and/or are sitting at that college graduation ceremony, will you be saying, I'm glad I did, or I wish I would have? (tip #129) I know which one I want to say.

Reach out to me on social media: Twitter: @andrewmarotta21 or on Facebook, Instagram, or LinkedIn. Would love to hear which tip was your favorite or most helpful to you. Also, please take and share the stories. I lived most of them and am happy to pass them on. Take them and use them to teach that lesson or make a memorable experience for your child. A few last points to remember:

- Do the best you can for your child and family and forget the rest.
- This is a marathon, not a sprint.
- You are not perfect: when you make mistakes, say sorry, and forgive yourself.
- Take care of yourself through this. You can't keep giving if you do not keep your bucket full. What do they say on the airplanes about the oxygen masks when they drop in an emergency? Put on your mask so you can breathe and then help others.
- What can you do that is the best for your kid(s)? Love their mother, father, guardian, or partner. Kids model what they see and feel. My best to you on your journey. #KeepRolling

Do your best and forget the rest. Thank you for reading. It was an honor to be with you! #SurviveThrive

INDEX

(1) LOVE

33. Problems they have in school may be the same or similar problems later in life.

34. ADD: Attention Deficit Disorder by Jennifer Marotta

35. Your kid might have a different experience than you did.

36. They are not too old for bedtime.

37. Hoot with the owls.

38. Focus on the effort, not the outcome. Focus on the process, not the result.

39. Organization, Organization, Organization

40. Planning it out by Denise Dicks

41. Have your child find a part-time job/summer job (preferably doing something they like).

42. If you do the crime, you do the time.

43. Nothing good happens after midnight.

44. Do you know where they are after school?

45. Don't curse: Smash the cassette story.

46. You never know who is on the other end of the call.

47. If you suspect drugs or alcohol, bring a strong, fast-acting response.

48. Is it difficult or just time-consuming?

49. Focus.

(4) TRUTHS

(5) SOCIAL & EMOTIONAL WELLNESS & THE POWER OF RESILIENCY

(10) PARENTING & COACHING

(11) CLOSING: GRATITUDE: THE HIGHEST VIRTUE

REFERENCES

Bettger, F. (1986). How I raised myself from failure to success in selling. *Prentice Hall Press.*

Billy, J. (2018). Lead with culture. *Dave Burgess Consulting, Inc.*

Bryan, L. (2018). Most people are good [Song]. On What Makes You Country. *Capitol Nashville.*

Halloween Wars *[Television Series]. (2020). Food Network.*

Cain, A., & Gillett, R. (2018). 11 Signs someone might be lying to you. Business Insider. *https://www. businessinsider.com/11-signs-someone-is-lying-2014-4*

Covey, S. R. (2004). The 7 habits of highly effective
people: Powerful lessons in personal change. *Free
Press.*

[@Dawsonbtaylor]. (2016, October 18). We need to
care less about whether our children are
academically gifted & more about whether they sit
with the *[Infographic]. Instagram. https://www.
instagram.com/p/BLsIT83jnQY/*

Doucette, D. [@thedanielledoucette]. (n.d.). Danielle
Doucette | The Kartra Coach *[Infographic].
Pinterest. https://www.pinterest.
com/pin/350928995962598758/*

*Freedman, J., Jensen, A.L., Rideout, M.C., &
Freedman, P.E. (1998). Handle with care:
Emotional intelligence activity book.* Six Seconds.

Gladwell, M. (2011). Outliers: The story of success
(1st ed.). *Back Bay Books.*

*Haas, S.B. (2018, April 17). 6 Ways that night-time
phone usage destroys your sleep.* Psychology
Today. *https://www.psychologytoday.com/us/blog/
prescriptions-life/201804/6-ways-night-time-
phone-use-destroys-your-sleep*

Hagner, L. (Host). (2018-present). The dad edge
podcast *[Audio podcast]. iTunes. https://
gooddadproject.com/podcast/*

Robbins, A. (2003). Unlimited power: The new science of personal achievement. *Free Press.*

Rockwell, D. (2020, November 30). *5 things I learned from 30 days of gratitude.* Leadership Freak. *Retrieved from https://leadershipfreak.blog/2020/ 11/30/5-things-i-learned-from-30-days-of- gratitude/*

Rockwell, D. (2018, August 31). *How to inspire others to fly.* Leadership Freak. *https://leadershipfreak. blog/2018/08/31/how-to-inspire-others-to-fly/*

Roffey, S. (2012). *Developing positive relationships in schools.* Positive relationships: Evidence-based practice across the world *(pp. 145-162). Springer Science+Business Media. DOI: 10.1007/978-94- 007-2147-0*

Roosevelt, T. (1910, April 23). Citizenship in a republic *[Speech]. Leadership Now. https://www. leadershipnow.com/tr-citizenship.html*

Sackey, A. (2020, November 10). *Time.* Breath of Faith. *Retrieved from https://breathoffaith.com/ blog/f/time*

Spainhour, D. (2018). Leading narratives: The perfect collection of stories, jokes, and wits of wisdom for leaders. *The Leadership Publishing Team.*

Spainhour, D. (2015, November). *Strategies, ideas, and news to help you lead your team.* The Coaching and Leadership Journal. *Retrieved from https://www.leadershippublishingteam.com/the-coaching-and-leadership-journal.html*

Springsteen, B. (2016). Born to run. *Simon & Schuster Paperbacks.*

Stevenson, D. (n.d.). Doc Deana Enterprises, LLC: About us. *https://docdeanaenterprises.com/about-dde*

The Beatles. (1967). *All you need is love [Song]. Parlophone; Capitol.*

Thorne, J.D. (2009). The 10 commandments of baseball: An affectionate look at Joe McCarty's principles for success in baseball (and life). *Sporting Chance Press.*

TV commercials. (2017, August 19). Apple - misunderstood (2013) - Christmas commercial *[Video]. YouTube. https://youtu.be/Og637tBf91s*

VelocityFilmsOnline. (2014, March 14). Bells - Reader directed by Greg Gray *[Video]. YouTube. https://youtu.be/Yy7fxLwfOnQ*

Andrew Marotta is the enthused and energetic Principal at Port Jervis High School located in beautiful Port Jervis, NY. Under his collaborative leadership, Port Jervis HS has grown in many areas, including academic achievement, student success, and most importantly, a culture of #PortPride. He loves his school community and continues to #survivethrive in his efforts to continue to move things forward.

Andrew is supported by his loving family, his wife Jennifer, and his children Claire, Matthew, and Tessa. So many experiences in this book are from Andrew's role as a Principal, a son, and his favorite role, being a dad to his wonderful children. He is so grateful for his family and loves them unconditionally.

In addition to *The Partnership,* Andrew has authored his first book, *The Principal, Surviving and Thriving* in 2017, 2nd edition, *The School Leader,* in 2020. These books have propelled Andrew to become a national speaker and presenter on leadership, relationship building, and the points of his logo: energy, enthusiasm, effort, extra, all leading to excellence. He is a master storyteller who brings his audiences to laugh, cry, think, reflect, and more.

Learn more about Andrew at https://andrewmarotta.com/ Sign up for his weekly leadership blog #ELBlog on his website and watch his podcast on social media #ELB Education Leadership and Beyond. He truly is AlottaMarotta! #SurviveThrive

EduMatch Publishing

Made in the USA
Middletown, DE
24 May 2021